# THE VOCAL LIBRARY

# Franz Schubert
# 15 Selected Songs

## High Voice

edited by Richard Walters

Martha Gerhart, translations and International Phonetic Alphabet
Irene Spiegelman, diction coach
Laura Ward, pianist

To access companion recorded accompaniments
and diction lessons online, visit:
**www.halleonard.com/mylibrary**

Enter Code
8337-0285-0076-4574

Editions of some of the songs in this collection, including historical notes and translations,
were previously published in the following Hal Leonard Vocal Library titles:

*The Lieder Anthology*
Edited by Virginia Saya and Richard Walters

*Favorite German Art Songs*

*Favorite German Art Songs, Volume 2*

*Franz Schubert: 100 Songs*
Edited by Steven Stolen and Richard Walters

Cover painting: Leopold Kupelwieser, *Ball Games at Atzenbrugg with Franz Schubert* (1797–1828) *and friends seated in the foreground*,
pen and ink and watercolor on paper, Gesellschaft der Musikfreunde, Vienna, Austria
© The Bridgeman Art Library/Getty Images

ISBN 978-1-4234-4665-1

# HAL•LEONARD®
## CORPORATION
7777 W. BLUEMOUND RD. P.O. BOX 13819 MILWAUKEE, WI 53213

In Australia Contact:
**Hal Leonard Australia Pty. Ltd.**
4 Lentara Court
Cheltenham, Victoria, 3192 Australia
Email: ausadmin@halleonard.com.au

Visit Hal Leonard Online at
**www.halleonard.com**

# Contents

# Franz Schubert

The talents of Franz Schubert are well chronicled in any music history source. His nine symphonies, choral pieces, and countless piano and chamber works make him, of course, a major European musical figure, particularly as a transitory talent from the Classical to the Romantic. It is, however, his work as a song composer, producing some 600-plus lieder, which grants him a unique place in history. His song composition began at least as early as age 14 and continued until his death, with some periods of enormous output. In the two-year period of 1815 and 1816 he wrote a remarkable 250 songs.

Schubert re-invented the lied, going much further in the endeavor of setting poetry to music than anyone before him. He created the first substantial body of literature for the vocal recital. His accomplishment, however great, could not have happened without the rise of German lyric poetry by Johann Wolfgang von Goethe, Heinrich Heine, Wilhelm Müller, Ludwig Rellstab, Friedrich Rückert, and Johann Christoph Friedrich von Schiller during the late 18th century and first decades of the 19th century. Schubert also set texts by many more literary minor figures, some of which were friends.

Musical success during Schubert's lifetime was measured against Beethoven in the concert hall and Rossini in the opera house. Schubert dreamed of triumph in both places, but never achieved it, almost always failing to find performances of his larger works. As an alternative, the devoted circle of friends around the composer would gather in living rooms and parlors for evenings which came to be called Schubertiads. A majority of the songs were first performed there. These evenings encouraged Schubert in song composition, since there was a ready place, performers and audience for the works. The composer was at the piano regularly in the Schubertiads, accompanying songs and playing piano pieces, but never performed for a wider public. His piano abilities seem to have been adequate but not remarkable. Schubert had many favorite singers, lyric baritone Johann Michael Vogl and soprano Anna Milder Hauptmann among them. On occasion Schubert himself sang a new song for the intimate Schubertiad audience, though he never would have considered himself a singer.

Schubert explored various musical forms in his songs, including strophic, through-composed, freely declamatory, and combined structures. His text setting shines with a balance of sensitivity to words and strong melodic values. The piano accompaniment figures imaginatively reflect the mood and imagery of the texts. Among Schubert's achievements as a song composer is the full flowering of the concept of a narrative song cycle, a group of related poems which tell some kind of story by their progression, shown in the expansive sets *Die Winterreise* and *Die schöne Müllerin*.

Schubert's composition was inspired by many influences. He loved the operas of Gluck, and discovered the baritone Vogl at a performance of *Iphigénie en Tauride*. Schubert also greatly admired Handel, and in his free time played through that composer's operas and oratorios. He thought Mozart's *Don Giovanni* among the very best of all operas, and valued the overture to *Die Zauberflöte* as a masterwork with few peers. As for Beethoven, Schubert held him in high regard. Though they both lived in Vienna, the two never met until 1827, and then briefly, with Beethoven virtually on his deathbed. Five years earlier Schubert dedicated a set of published piano variations to Beethoven and brought a copy to him. The great and famous man was not at home, and humbled by the idea of a return visit, Schubert simply left the new edition. Beethoven apparently approved of the music, and played it nearly every day thereafter with his nephew.

Richard Walters
editor

# About the Artists

**Martha Gerhart** relocated to Dallas, Texas in 1997, following a prestigious career as a coach/pianist based in New York City, to teach at Southern Methodist University. At S.M.U. she coaches and teaches Diction for Singers. In demand from both students and professionals in the Dallas-Fort Worth area at her private coaching studio in Dallas, she has been on the music staffs of companies including the New York City Opera, the San Francisco Opera, Spoleto Festival Opera, and The Dallas Opera. She has also presented master classes at venues including the Pittsburgh Opera Studio, Glimmerglass Opera, OperaWorks (Los Angeles), and the Texoma Regional NATS Convention. In addition to her translating and IPA transliterating contributions to G. Schirmer's *Opera Anthology* series and other publications, she is the author of *Italian song texts from the 17th through the 20th centuries*, in three volumes, published by Leyerle Publications.

Born in Germany, raised and educated in West Berlin, **Irene Spiegelman** earned undergraduate and graduate degrees in English literature, drama, and pedagogy. She moved to the US in 1975 and later earned a Ph.D. from New York University specializing in 19th century German literature.

Spiegelman is the German coach at the Metropolitan Opera, a position she has held since 1977. She also teaches and coaches German for the Met's Lindemann Young Artist Development Program. She edited the German titles for the new multi-lingual Met Titles, which were introduced in the 2006–07 season.

Specializing in interpretation, diction, and spoken dialogues, she is a private coach for many renowned opera singers. Spiegelman has also coached for the New York Philharmonic and Wolf Trap Opera. She assisted in opera recordings for Sony Classical, Decca, and Deutsche Grammophon. Since 2004, she has been invited to the Marlboro Summer Music Festival to work on the lieder repertoire of promising young singers.

**Laura Ward** has been a vocal coach and collaborative pianist at the Washington Opera, the Academy of Vocal Arts, the Ravinia Festival, the Music Academy of the West, the Blossom Festival, the University of Maryland, and Temple University. Laura has been the official pianist for the Washington International Vocal competition and the Marian Anderson Award. She has performed at several international music festivals such as the Spoleto Festival in Spoleto, Italy, and the Colmar International Music Festival and Saint Denis Festival in France. A native of Texas, Laura received her Bachelor of Music degree from Baylor University, Master of Music degree in Piano Accompanying at the Cincinnati College-Conservatory of Music, and a Doctor of Musical Arts in Piano Accompanying from the University of Michigan with Martin Katz. There she was pianist for the Contemporary Directions Ensemble and she performed with the Ann Arbor Symphony. She is co-editor of *Richard Strauss: 40 Songs, Gabriel Fauré: 50 Songs,* and *Johannes Brahms: 75 Songs,* all Hal Leonard publications in *The Vocal Library* series. She is co-founder and pianist for Lyric Fest, a dynamic and innovative recital series in Philadelphia. Laura has recorded more accompaniments than any other pianist, with well over two thousand tracks to her credit. Her recordings include twenty volumes in *The First Book of Solos* series (G. Schirmer), eight volumes of *Easy Songs for Beginning Singers* (G. Schirmer), *28 Italian Songs and Arias of the Seventeenth and Eighteenth Centuries, The First Book of Broadway Solos* series (four volumes, Hal Leonard), five volumes of *Standard Vocal Literature* (Hal Leonard, *The Vocal Library*), over twenty other volumes in *The Vocal Library, The New Imperial Edition* (six volumes, Boosey & Hawkes), and various other collections.

# About the Recordings

Veteran diction coach Irene Spiegelman is a native German speaker whose specialty is working with classical singers, particularly at the Metropolitan Opera. This book/audio package allows a student access to German diction coaching at the highest level.

There are two recordings of each song text. First, the coach recites the poem. A singer can hear the mood of the text and the flow of the language. It is important to remember that this poem is what inspired the composer to write an art song setting. Spoken diction is used in the recitation, including the guttural "R" sound in German. However, even in the recitation the coach is aware of how the words were set to music.

Next, the coach has recorded the text line-by-line, without expression, leaving time for the repetition of each phrase. In this slow version the guttural "R" sound has been adapted to the flipped "R" recommended for classical singers. Other small adjustments have been made relevant to the manner in which the words are set to music.

To achieve the best artistic results, it is crucial that the singer spends time with the poem apart from singing it, not only mastering diction to the point of fluency, but also in contemplating the words and learning to express their meanings. Is there an implied character speaking the poem? Only after a singer has pondered the words can she or he appreciate and discern how the composer interpreted the poetry, which is the heart of what art song is.

We make every effort to record a high quality, artistically satisfying accompaniment. Pianist Laura Ward has a deep understanding of the repertory and is extremely experienced in working with singers, from students to professionals. The nature of recording forces one to make one choice in interpretation and tempo. The phrasing implied in any of these piano accompaniment recordings and the recorded tempo should be considered by the singer. However, there is certainly not one way to interpret any art song. We are fully aware that there are other choices beyond those recorded. Ultimately, a singer should use the accompaniment recordings as a learning tool, for practice only, before moving on to working with a pianist, at which time adjustments in tempo and other nuances can and should be explored.

Richard Walters
editor

# TABLE
## of the International Phonetic Alphabet (IPA) symbols

### for the pronunciation of German in singing
### used in this Diction Guide

### The Vowels

| symbol | equivalent in English | description |
|---|---|---|
| [ɑː] | as in "father" | long (or "dark") "a" |
| [a] | similar to the first element in "ice" | short (or "bright") "a" |
| [eː] | no equivalent; similar to the first element in "gate" | long and closed "e" : [iː] in the [ɛ] position |
| [e] | as in "gate," but | short and closed "e" when in *articles* |
| [ɛ] | as in "bet" | short and open "e" |
| [ɛː] | as in the first element of "may" | long sound of "ä" |
| [ə] | approximately as in "approve" | neutral sound (the "schwa"): slightly darker than [ɛ]; appears only in unstressed syllables |
| [ʁ] | no equivalent | a variant of [ə], in place of the flipped "r"; to be used judiciously at the end of words such as "der," "mir," and etc., depending on the musical setting* |
| [iː] | as in "feet" | long and closed "i" |
| [i] | as in "feet," but | short and closed when in *articles* |
| [ɪ] | as in "bit" | short and open "i" |
| [oː] | no equivalent; approximately as in "boat | long and closed "o" |
| [o] | as in "boat," but | short and closed in some words |
| [ɔ] | as in "ought" | short and open "o" |
| [uː] | as in "blue" | long and closed "u" |
| [ʊ] | as in "put" | short and open "u" |
| [u] | as in "blue," but | short and closed in some words |
| [yː] | no equivalent | "y" or "ü" : long and closed; [iː] with the lips rounded |
| [ʏ] | no equivalent | "y" : short and open; [ɪ] with the lips rounded |
| [øː] | no equivalent | "ö" : long and closed; [eː] with the lips rounded |
| [œ] | as in "girl" without the "rl" | "ö" : short and open; [ɛ] with the lips rounded |

*While recommended use is reflected in these transliterations, the singer is always "correct" to use the flipped "r."

### The Diphthongs

| | |
|---|---|
| [ɑo] | similar to "house" in English |
| [ae] | similar to "mine" in English |
| [ɔø] | similar to "hoist" in English |

Diphthongs are transliterated with a slur over them (example: a͡o )

## The Consonants

| | | |
|---|---|---|
| [b] | bad | becomes unvoiced [p] at the end of a word or word element |
| [d] | door | becomes unvoiced [t] at the end of a word or word element |
| [f] | fine | also the sound of "v" in some words |
| [g] | go | becomes unvoiced [k] at the end of a word or word element |
| [ʒ] | vision | also the sound of initial "j" in words of French origin |
| [h] | hand | pronounced at the beginning of a word or word element |
| [j] | yes | except when pronounced [ʒ] (see above) |
| [k] | kite | also the sound of "g" at the end of a word or word element |
| [l] | lit | |
| [m] | mine | |
| [n] | no | |
| [ŋ] | sing | |
| [p] | pass | see also [b], above |
| [r] | no equivalent | flipped (or occasionally rolled, for dramatic reasons) "r" * |
| [s] | sing | before a consonant (except for the initial combinations "sp" and "st") and at the end of a word or word element; also the sound of "β," called the "Eszett," recently declared antiquated in German spelling. |
| [ʃ] | shoe | in the single element "sch"; also in the combination [tʃ], pronounced as in cheese |
| [t] | tip | see also [d], above |
| [v] | vase, or feel | depending on various word origins |
| [w] | vet | |
| [z] | bits | but pronounced as [z] when before a vowel and in some other circumstances; also, the sound of "s" in many words |
| [ç] | no equivalent | the "ich laut": following a "front vowel" or a consonant |
| [χ] | no equivalent | the "ach laut": following a "back vowel" |

*The "uvular 'r'" used in German conversation and popular song is not appropriate in classical art song and opera.

## Diacritical Marks

| | | |
|---|---|---|
| [:] | following a vowel = | that vowel is long |
| ['] | preceding a syllable = | the following syllable has the primary stress |
| [ˌ] | preceding a syllable = | the following syllable has the secondary stress |

The transliterations provided in this Guide do not include diacritical markings to indicate a recommended "glottal stroke" – a new "attack" of articulation on the following vowel – which are provided in some sources by the symbol [|].

    (example with the diacritical marking: ganz allein = [gants la ˈla͡en])

Many instances of the need for a "glottal stroke" will be obvious to the singer, guided by coaches and teachers; other instances are variable, and the practice should not be overdone.

As an additional aid for the user, syllables are separated by spaces in the IPA transliterations.

*– Martha Gerhart*

## An die Musik

an    di:    mu ˈzik
**An    die    Musik**
to    the    music

du:    ˈhɔl də    kʊnst    ɪn    ˈvi: fi:l    ˈgrao ən    ˈʃtʊn dən
**Du    holde    Kunst,    in    wieviel    grauen    Stunden,**
you    lovely    art    in    how many    grey    hours

vo:    mɪç    dɛs    ˈle: bəns    ˈvɪl dəʁ    kraes    ʊm ˈʃtrɪkt
**wo    mich    des    Lebens    wilder    Kreis    umstrickt,**
where    me    of    life    wild    circle    ensnares

hast    du:    maen    hɛrts    tsu:    ˈvar məʁ    li:p    ɛnt ˈtsʊn dən
**hast    du    mein    Herz    zu    warmer    Lieb    entzunden,**
have    you    my    heart    to    warmer    love    kindled

hast    mɪç    ɪn    ˈae nə    ˈbɛs rə    vɛlt    ɛnt ˈrʏkt
**hast    mich    in    eine    bessre    Welt    entrückt.**
have (you)    me    to    a    better    world    carried away

ɔft    hat    aen    ˈzɔøf tsər    ˈdae nər    harf    ɛnt ˈflɔ sən
**Oft    hat    ein    Seufzer,    deiner    Harf    entflossen,**
often    has    a    sigh    from your    harp    emanated

aen    ˈzy: sər    ˈhae lɪ gər    a ˈkɔrt    fɔn    di:ʁ
**ein    süßer,    heiliger    Akkord    von    dir,**
a    sweet    holy    chord    from    you

den    ˈhɪ məl    ˈbɛs rəʁ    ˈtsae tən    mi:r    ɛʁ ˈʃlɔ sən
**den    Himmel    bessrer    Zeiten    mir    erschlossen,**
the    heaven    of better    times    to me    opened up

du:    ˈhɔl də    kʊnst    ɪç    ˈdaŋ kə    di:ʁ    da ˈfy:ʁ
**du    holde    Kunst,    ich    danke    dir    dafür,**
you    lovely    art    I    thank    you    in return for it

du:    ˈhɔl də    kʊnst    ɪç    ˈdaŋ kə    di:ʁ
**du    holde    Kunst,    ich    danke    dir.**
you    lovely    art    I    thank    you

## An die Nachtigall

an     di:     ˈnaχ ti gal
**An    die    Nachtigall**
To    the    Nightingale

eːʁ   liːkt  ʊnt  ʃlɛːft  an  ˈma͡e nəm  ˈhɛr tsən
**Er   liegt  und  schläft  an  meinem  Herzen,**
he   lies  and  sleeps  at  my  heart

ma͡en  ˈgu təʁ  ˈʃʊts ga͡est  zaŋ  iːn  a͡en
**mein  guter  Schutzgeist  sang  ihn  ein;**
my  good  guardian spirit  sang  him  to sleep

ʊnt  ɪç  kan  ˈfrø lɪç  za͡en  ʊnt  ˈʃɛr tsən
**und  ich  kann  fröhlich  sein  und  scherzen,**
and  I  can  merry  be  and  joke

kan  ˈje: dəʁ  bluːm  ʊnt  ˈje: dəs  blats  mɪç  frɔ͡øn
**kann  jeder  Blum  und  jedes  Blatts  mich  freun.**
[I] can  of every  flower  and  every  leaf  myself  delight in

ˈnaχ ti gal  aχ  ˈnaχ ti gal  aχ
**Nachtigall,  ach!  Nachtigall,  ach!**
nightingale  ah  nightingale  ah

sɪŋ  miːʁ  deːn  ˈa: mor  nɪçt  vaχ
**Sing  mir  den  Amor  nicht  wach!**
sing  to me  the  Love  not  awake

# Auf dem Wasser zu singen

| ɑ͡of | dem | 'va sɐ | tsu: | 'zɪ ŋən |
|---|---|---|---|---|
| **Auf** | **dem** | **Wasser** | **zu** | **singen** |
| upon | the | water | for | to sing |

| 'mɪ tən | ɪm | 'ʃlɪ mɐ | de:ʁ | 'ʃpi: gəln dən | 've lən |
|---|---|---|---|---|---|
| **Mitten** | **im** | **Schimmer** | **der** | **spiegelnden** | **Wellen** |
| middle (of) | in the | shimmer | of the | reflecting | waves |

| 'glɑ͡e tət | vi: | 'ʃvɛ: nə | de:ʁ | 'vaŋ kən də | kɑ:n |
|---|---|---|---|---|---|
| **gleitet,** | **wie** | **Schwäne,** | **der** | **wankende** | **Kahn.** |
| glides | like | swans | the | wavering | boat |

| aχ | ɑ͡of | de:ʁ | 'frɔ͡ø də | zanft | 'ʃɪ mɐn dən | 've lən |
|---|---|---|---|---|---|---|
| **Ach,** | **auf** | **der** | **Freude** | **sanft** | **schimmernden** | **Wellen** |
| ah | on | of the | joy | soft | shimmering | waves |

| 'glɑ͡e tət | di: | 'ze: lə | da 'hɪn | vi: | de:ʁ | kɑ:n |
|---|---|---|---|---|---|---|
| **gleitet** | **die** | **Seele** | **dahin** | **wie** | **der** | **Kahn.** |
| glides | the | soul | along | like | the | boat |

| dɛn | fɔn | de:m | 'hɪ məl | hɛ 'rap | ɑ͡of | di: | 've lən |
|---|---|---|---|---|---|---|---|
| **Denn** | **von** | **dem** | **Himmel** | **herab** | **auf** | **die** | **Wellen** |
| for | from | the | heaven | downward | upon | the | waves |

| 'tan tsət | das | 'ɑ: bənt ˌro:t | rʊnt | ʊm | de:n | kɑ:n |
|---|---|---|---|---|---|---|
| **tanzet** | **das** | **Abendrot** | **rund** | **um** | **den** | **Kahn.** |
| dances | the | sunset | round | about | the | boat |

| 'y: bɐ | de:n | 'vɪp fəln | dɛs | 'vɛst lɪ çən | 'hɑ͡e nəs |
|---|---|---|---|---|---|
| **Über** | **den** | **Wipfeln** | **des** | **westlichen** | **Haines** |
| over | the | treetops | of the | western | grove |

| 'vɪŋ kət | ʊns | 'frɔ͡ønt lɪç | de:ʁ | 'rø:t lɪ çə | ʃɑ͡en |
|---|---|---|---|---|---|
| **winket** | **uns** | **freundlich** | **der** | **rötliche** | **Schein.** |
| beckons | to us | friendly | the | reddish | sheen |

| 'ʊn tɐ | de:n | 'tsvɑ͡e gən | dɛs | 'œst lɪ çən | 'hɑ͡e nəs |
|---|---|---|---|---|---|
| **Unter** | **den** | **Zweigen** | **des** | **östlichen** | **Haines** |
| under | the | branches | of the | eastern | grove |

| 'zɔ͡ø zəlt | de:ʁ | 'kal mʊs | ɪm | 'rø:t lɪ çən | ʃɑ͡en |
|---|---|---|---|---|---|
| **säuselt** | **der** | **Kalmus** | **im** | **rötlichen** | **Schein.** |
| russles | the | calamus | in the | reddish | sheen |

| 'frɔ͡ø də | dɛs | 'hɪ məls | ʊnt | 'ru: ə | dɛs | 'hɑ͡e nəs |
|---|---|---|---|---|---|---|
| **Freude** | **des** | **Himmels** | **und** | **Ruhe** | **des** | **Haines** |
| joy | of the | heaven | and | peace | of the | grove |

| 'ɑ:t mət | di: | ze:l | ɪm | ɛʁ 'rø: tən dən | ʃɑ͡en |
|---|---|---|---|---|---|
| **atmet** | **die** | **Seel** | **im** | **errötenden** | **Schein.** |
| breathes | the | soul | in the | reddening | glow |

| aχ | ɛs | ɛnt 'ʃvɪn dət | mɪt | 'tɑ͡o i gəm | 'fly: gəl |
|---|---|---|---|---|---|
| **Ach,** | **es** | **entschwindet** | **mit** | **tauigem** | **Flügel** |
| ah | it | vanishes | with | dewy | wing |

| mi:ɐ | ɑ͡of | den | 'vi: gən dən | 've lən | di: | tsɑ͡et |
|---|---|---|---|---|---|---|
| **mir** | **auf** | **den** | **wiegenden** | **Wellen** | **die** | **Zeit.** |
| to me | upon | the | rocking | waves | the | time |

| 'mɔr gən | ɛnt 'ʃvɪn dət | mɪt | 'ʃɪ mɐn dəm | 'fly: gəl |
|---|---|---|---|---|
| **Morgen** | **entschwindet** | **mit** | **schimmerndem** | **Flügel** |
| tomorrow | vanishes | with | shimmering | wing |

| 'vi: dɐ | vi: | 'ge stɐn | ʊnt | 'hɔ͡ø tə | di: | tsɑ͡et |
|---|---|---|---|---|---|---|
| **wieder** | **wie** | **gestern** | **und** | **heute** | **die** | **Zeit,** |
| again | like | yesterday | and | today | the | time |

| bɪs | ɪç | ɑ͡of | 'hø: ə rəm | 'ʃtrɑ: lən dən | 'fly: gəl |
|---|---|---|---|---|---|
| **bis** | **ich** | **auf** | **höherem** | **strahlenden** | **Flügel** |
| until | I | on | loftier | radiant | wing |

| 'zɛl bɐ | ɛnt 'ʃvɪn də | de:ʁ | 'vɛk səln dən | tsɑ͡et |
|---|---|---|---|---|
| **selber** | **entschwinde** | **der** | **wechselnden** | **Zeit.** |
| myself | vanish | to the | changing | time |

## Der Musensohn

deːʁ 'muː zən ˌzoːn
**Der Musensohn**
the muses' son

dʊrç fɛlt ʊnt valt tsuː 'ʃvae fən
**Durch Feld und Wald zu schweifen,**
through field and forest to roam

maen 'liː tçən 'vɛk tsuː ˌpfae fən
**mein Liedchen wegzupfeifen,**
my little song away to whistle

zoː geːts fɔn ɔrt tsuː ɔrt
**so geht's von Ort zu Ort.**
so goes it from place to place

ʊnt naːχ deːm 'tak tə 're gət
**Und nach dem Takte reget**
and to the beat animates

ʊnt naːχ deːm maːs bə 'veː gət
**und nach dem Maß beweget**
and to the measure moves

zɪç 'a ləs an miːʁ fɔrt
**sich alles an mir fort.**
itself everything by me forth

ɪç kan ziː kaom ɛʁ 'var tən
**Ich kann sie kaum erwarten,**
I can them scarcely wait for

diː 'eːr stə bluːm ɪm 'gar tən
**die erste Blum im Garten,**
the first flower in the garden

diː 'eːr stə blyːt am baom
**die erste Blüt am Baum.**
the first bloom on the tree

ziː 'gryː sən 'mae nə 'liː dəʁ
**Sie grüßen meine Lieder,**
they greet my songs

ʊnt kɔmt deːʁ 'vɪn təʁ 'viː dəʁ
**und kommt der Winter wieder,**
and (when) comes the winter again

zɪŋ ɪç nɔχ 'je nən traom
**sing ich noch jenen Traum.**
sing I still that dream

ɪç zɪŋ iːn ɪn deːʁ 'vae tə
**Ich sing ihn in der Weite,**
I sing it in the distance

aof 'ae zəs lɛŋ ʊnt 'brae tə
**auf Eises Läng' und Breite,**
on of ice length and breadth

daː blyːt deːʁ 'vɪn təʁ ʃøːn
**da blüht der Winter schön.**
there blooms the winter beautiful

aoχ 'diː zə 'blyː tə 'ʃvɪn dət
**Auch diese Blüte schwindet,**
also this blossom disappears

ʊnt 'noø ə 'froø də 'fɪn dət
**und neue Freude findet**
and new joy finds

zɪç aof bə 'baø tən høːn
**sich auf bebauten Höhn.**
itself on cultivated hills

dɛn viː ɪç bae deːʁ 'lɪn də
**Denn wie ich bei der Linde**
then as I by the linden tree

das 'jʊ ŋə 'fœlk çən 'fɪn də
**das junge Völkchen finde,**
the young folk find

zoː 'glaeç ɛʁ 'reː gɪç ziː
**sogleich erreg ich sie.**
instantly excite I them

deːʁ 'ʃtʊm pfə 'bʊr ʃə blɛːt zɪç
**Der stumpfe Bursche bläht sich,**
the dull fellow puffs up himself

das 'ʃtae fə 'mɛːt çən dreːt zɪç
**das steife Mädchen dreht sich**
the stiff girl twirls herself

naːχ 'mae nər me lo 'diː
**nach meiner Melodie.**
to my melody

iːʁ geːpt den 'zoː lən 'flyː gəl
**Ihr gebt den Sohlen Flügel**
you give the soles wings

ʊnt traept dʊrç taːl ʊnt 'hyː gəl
**und treibt durch Tal und Hügel**
and drive through vale and hill

den 'liːp lɪŋ vaet fɔn haos
**den Liebling weit von Haus.**
the darling far from home

iːʁ 'liː bən 'hɔl dən 'muː zən
**Ihr lieben, holden Musen,**
you dear gracious muses

van ruː ɪç iːʁ am 'buː zən
**wann ruh ich ihr am Busen**
when repose I to her on the bosom

aoχ 'ɛnt lɪç 'viː dəʁ aos
**auch endlich wieder aus?**
also at last again — [upon; ausruhen, a separable verb, = to repose]

# Die Forelle

di: fo 'rɛ lə
**Die Forelle**
the trout

ɪn 'ae nəm 'bɛç laen 'hɛ lə
**In einem Bächlein helle,**
in a little brook clear

dɑ: ʃɔs ɪn 'fro: ɐ ael
**da schoss in froher Eil**
there darted in joyful haste

di: 'lao nɪ ʃə fo 'rɛ lə
**die launische Forelle**
the peevish trout

fo: 'ry: bəɐ vi: aen pfael
**vorüber wie ein Pfeil.**
along like an arrow

ɪç ʃtant an dem gə 'ʃtɑ: də
**Ich stand an dem Gestade**
I stood on the bank

ʊnt za: ɪn 'zy: sɐ ru:
**und sah in süßer Ruh**
and looked in sweet repose

dɛs 'mʊn tɐn 'fɪʃ laens 'bɑ: də
**des muntern Fischleins Bade**
of the merry little fish bath

ɪm 'klɑ: rən 'bɛç laen tsu:
**im klaren Bächlein zu.**
in the clear little brook at

aen 'fɪ ʃɐ mɪt de:ɐ 'ru: tə
**Ein Fischer mit der Rute**
A fisherman with the rod

vo:l an de:m 'ʊ: fɐ ʃtant
**wohl an dem Ufer stand**
indeed on the bank stood

ʊnt zɑ:s mɪt 'kal təm 'blu: tə
**und sah's mit kaltem Blute,**
and saw it with cold blood

vi: zɪç das 'fɪʃ laen vant
**wie sich das Fischlein wand.**
how itself the little fish wriggled

zo: laŋ de:m 'va sɐ 'hɛ lə
**So lang dem Wasser Helle,**
as long as to the water clearness

zo: daχt ɪç nɪçt gə 'brɪçt
**so dacht ich, nicht gebricht,**
so thought I not is lacking

zo: fɛŋt e:ɐ di: fo 'rɛ lə
**so fängt er die Forelle**
so catches he the trout

mɪt 'zae nɐ 'a ŋəl nɪçt
**mit seiner Angel nicht.**
with his fishing tackle not

dɔχ 'ɛnt lɪç vart dem 'di: bə
**Doch endlich ward dem Diebe**
but finally became for the thief

di: tsaet tsu: laŋ e:ɐ maχt
**die Zeit zu lang. Er macht**
the time too long He made

das 'bɛç laen 'tʏ kɪʃ 'try: bə
**das Bächlein tückisch trübe,**
the little brook malicious muddy

ʊnt e: ɪç ɛs gə 'daχt
**und eh ich es gedacht,**
and before I it realized

zo: 'tsʊk tə 'zae nə 'ru: tə
**so zuckte seine Rute,**
so (he) jerked his rod

das 'fɪʃ laen 'tsa pəlt dran
**das Fischlein zappelt dran,**
the little fish dangled thereon

ʊnt ɪç mɪt 're: gəm 'blu: tə
**und ich mit regem Blute**
and I with aroused blood

za: di: bə 'tro:g nə an
**sah die Betrogne an.**
looked the deceived one at

## Du bist die Ruh

du: bɪst di: ru:
**Du bist die Ruh,**
you are the repose

deːʁ ˈfriː də mɪlt
**der Friede mild,**
the peace gentle

di: ˈzeːn zʊχt du:
**die Sehnsucht du,**
the longing you

ʊnt vas zi: ʃtɪlt
**und was sie stillt.**
and that which it appeases

ɪç ˈvaeə diːr
**Ich weihe dir**
I consecrate to you

fɔl lʊst ʊnt ʃmɛrts
**voll Lust und Schmerz**
full (of) pleasure and pain

tsuːʁ ˈvoː nʊŋ hiːʁ
**zur Wohnung hier**
for dwelling place here

maen aok ʊnt hɛrts
**mein Aug und Herz.**
my eye and heart

keːr aen bae miːʁ
**Kehr ein bei mir,**
lodge in by me

ʊnt ˈʃliː sə du:
**und schließe du**
and close you

ʃtɪl ˈhɪn təʁ diːʁ
**still hinter dir**
quietly behind you

di: ˈpfɔr tən tsu:
**die Pforten zu.**
the gates shut

traep ˈan dəʁn ʃmɛrts
**Treib andern Schmerz**
drive other pain

aos ˈdiː zəʁ brʊst
**aus dieser Brust.**
out of this breast

fɔl zae diːs hɛrts
**Voll sei dies Herz**
full be this heart

fɔn ˈdae nəʁ lʊst
**von deiner Lust.**
of your pleasure

diːs ˈao gən ˌtsɛlt
**Dies Augenzelt,**
this eyes' tabernacle

fɔn ˈdae nəm glants
**von deinem Glanz**
from your radiance

a ˈlaen ɛʁ ˈhɛlt
**allein erhellt,**
only brightens

oː fʏl ɛs gants
**o füll es ganz.**
oh fill it completely

# Ganymed

'gaː ny meːt
**Ganymed**
Ganymede

viː ɪm 'mɔr gən ˌglan tsə
**Wie im Morgenglanze**
how in the morning splendor

duː rɪŋs mɪç 'an glyːst
**du rings mich anglühst,**
you all around me glow at

'fryː lɪŋ gə 'liːp təʁ
**Frühling, Geliebter!**
spring beloved

mɪt 'taͨo zənt ˌfa χəʁ 'liː bəs ˌvɔ nə
**Mit tausendfacher Liebeswonne**
with thousandfold rapture of love

sɪç an maͨen 'hɛr tsə drɛŋt
**sich an mein Herze drängt**
itself to my heart presses

'daͨe nəʁ 'eː vɪ gən 'vɛr mə
**deiner ewigen Wärme**
of your eternal warmth

'haͨe lɪç gə 'fyːl
**heilig Gefühl,**
holy feeling

ʊn 'ɛnt lɪ çə 'ʃøː nə
**unendliche Schöne!**
unending beauty

das ɪç dɪç 'fa sən mœçt
**Dass ich dich fassen möcht**
that I you [to] clasp [I] might

ɪn 'diː zən arm
**in diesen Arm!**
in this arm

aχ an 'daͨe nəm 'buː zən
**Ach, an deinem Busen**
ah at your bosom

liːk ɪç ʊnt 'ʃmaχ tə
**lieg ich, und schmachte,**
lie I and [I] languish

ʊnt 'daͨe nə 'bluː mən daͨen graːs
**und deine Blumen, dein Gras**
and your flowers your grass

'drɛ ŋən sɪç an maͨen hɛrts
**drängen sich an mein Herz.**
press themselves at my heart

duː kyːlst deːn 'brɛ nən dən
**Du kühlst den brennenden**
you cool the burning

dʊrst 'maͨe nəs 'buː zəns
**Durst meines Busens,**
thirst of my bosom

'liːp lɪç əʁ 'mɔr gən vɪnt
**lieblicher Morgenwind!**
lovely morning breeze

ruːft draͨen diː 'naχ ti gal
**Ruft drein die Nachtigall**
calls therein the nightingale

'liː bənt naːχ miːʁ aͨos deːm 'neː bəl taːl
**liebend nach mir aus dem Nebeltal.**
lovingly to me from the mist valley

ɪç kɔm ɪç 'kɔ mə
**Ich komm! ich komme!**
I come I come

aχ vo 'hɪn vo 'hɪn
**Ach! wohin? wohin?**
ah whither whither

hɪ 'naͨof ʃtreːpts hɪ 'naͨof
**Hinauf strebt's, hinauf!**
upward strives it upward

ɛs 'ʃveː bən diː 'vɔl kən
**Es schweben die Wolken**
there float the clouds

'ap vɛrts diː 'vɔl kən
**abwärts, die Wolken**
downward the clouds

'naͨe gən zɪç deːʁ 'zeː nən dən 'liː bə
**neigen sich der sehnenden Liebe.**
bend down themselves to the yearning love

miːʁ miːʁ
**Mir! Mir!**
to me to me

ɪn 'ɔͨø rəm 'ʃoː sə
**In eurem Schoße**
in your lap

'aͨof vɛrts
**Aufwärts!**
upward

ʊm 'fa ŋənt ʊm 'fa ŋən
**Umfangend umfangen!**
embracing embraced

'aͨof vɛrts an 'daͨe nən 'buː zən
**Aufwärts an deinen Busen,**
upward to your bosom

al 'liː bən dəʁ 'fa təʁ
**allliebender Vater!**
all-loving Father

# Gretchen am Spinnrade

'gre: tçən   am      'ʃpɪn ra: də
**Gretchen    am       Spinnrade**
Gretchen    at the   spinning wheel

'mae nə   ru:    ɪst   hɪn
**Meine     Ruh    ist   hin,**
my        peace  is    gone

maen   hɛrts   ɪst   ʃve:ʁ
**mein   Herz    ist   schwer,**
my     heart   is    heavy

ɪç   'fɪn də   zi:   'nɪ məʁ
**ich  finde     sie   nimmer**
I    find       it    never

ʊnt   'nɪ məʁ ˌme:ʁ
**und    nimmermehr.**
and    nevermore

vo:   ɪç   i:n   nɪçt   ha:p
**Wo    ich  ihn   nicht  hab,**
where I    him   not    have

ɪst   mi:ʁ   das   gra:p
**ist   mir    das   Grab,**
is    to me  the   grave

di:   'gan tsə   vɛlt
**die   ganze      Welt**
the   whole      world

ɪst   mi:ʁ   fɛʁ 'gɛlt
**ist   mir    vergällt.**
is    to me  made bitter

maen   'ar məʁ   kɔpf
**Mein   armer     Kopf**
my     poor      head

ɪst   mi:ʁ   fɛʁ 'rʏkt
**ist   mir    verrückt,**
is    to me  deranged

maen   'ar məʁ   zɪn
**mein   armer     Sinn**
my     poor      mind

ɪst   mi:r   tsɛʁ 'ʃtʏkt
**ist   mir    zerstückt.**
is    to me  torn to pieces

naχ   i:m   nu:ʁ   ʃao   ɪç
**Nach  ihm   nur    schau  ich**
for   him   only   look  I

tsʊm   'fɛn stəʁ   hɪ 'naos
**zum    Fenster     hinaus,**
at the window      out

naχ   i:m   nu:ʁ   ge:   ɪç
**nach  ihm   nur    geh   ich**
for   him   only   go    I

aos   dem   haos
**aus   dem   Haus.**
out   of the house

zaen   'ho: əʁ   gaŋ
**Sein   hoher     Gang,**
his    proud     carriage

zaen   'e:d lə   gə 'ʃtalt
**sein'  edle      Gestalt,**
his    noble     stature

'zae nəs   'mʊn dəs   'lɛ çəln
**seines     Mundes     Lächeln,**
of his     mouth      smile

'zae nəʁ   'ao gən   gə 'valt
**seiner     Augen     Gewalt,**
of his     eyes      power

ʊnt   'zae nəʁ   're: də
**Und   seiner     Rede**
and   of his     words

'tsao bəʁ ˌflʊs
**Zauberfluss,**
magic flow

zaen   'hɛn də ˌdrʊk
**sein   Händedruck,**
his    hand clasp

ʊnt   aχ   zaen   kʊs
**und   ach,  sein   Kuss!**
and   ah   his    kiss

maen   'bu: zən   drɛŋt
**Mein   Busen      drängt**
my     bosom      urges

zɪç   na:χ   i:m   hɪn
**sich  nach   ihm   hin,**
itself toward him  thither

aχ   dʏrft         ɪç   'fa sən
**ach  dürft'        ich  fassen**
ah   might be allowed  I   to grasp

ʊnt   'hal tən   i:n
**und   halten     ihn,**
and   to hold    him

ʊnt   'kʏ sən   i:n
**und   küssen    ihn,**
and   to kiss   him

zo:   vi:   ɪç   vɔlt
**so    wie   ich  wollt',**
as    how   I    would

an   'zae nən   'kʏ sən
**an   seinen     Küssen**
at   his        kisses

fɛʁ 'ge: ən   zɔlt
**vergehen      sollt'.**
die           (I) should

# Heidenröslein

'hae dən ˌrøːs laen
**Heidenröslein**
Little Heath Rose

| za: | aen | knaːp | aen | 'røːs laen | ʃteːn |
|---|---|---|---|---|---|
| **Sah** | **ein** | **Knab** | **ein** | **Röslein** | **stehn,** |
| saw | a | boy | a | little rose | stand |

| 'røːs laen | aof | deːʁ | 'hae dən |
|---|---|---|---|
| **Röslein** | **auf** | **der** | **Heiden,** |
| little rose | on | the | heath |

| vaːʁ | zoː | jʊŋ | ʊnt | 'mɔr gən ʃøːn |
|---|---|---|---|---|
| **war** | **so** | **jung** | **und** | **morgenschön,** |
| [it] was | so | young | and | morning-beautiful |

| liːf | eːʁ | ʃnɛl | ɛs | naː | tsu | zeːn |
|---|---|---|---|---|---|---|
| **lief** | **er** | **schnell,** | **es** | **nah** | **zu** | **sehn,** |
| ran | he | quickly | it | near | to | [to] see |

| zaːs | mɪt | 'fiː lən | 'frɔø dən |
|---|---|---|---|
| **sah's** | **mit** | **vielen** | **Freuden.** |
| saw it | with | many | joys |

| 'røːs laen | 'røːs laen | 'røːs laen | roːt |
|---|---|---|---|
| **Röslein,** | **Röslein,** | **Röslein** | **rot,** |
| little rose | little rose | little rose | red |

| 'røːs laen | aof | deːʁ | 'hae dən |
|---|---|---|---|
| **Röslein** | **auf** | **der** | **Heiden.** |
| little rose | on | the | heath |

| 'knaː bə | ʃpraːχ | ɪç | 'brɛ çə | dɪç |
|---|---|---|---|---|
| **Knabe** | **sprach:** | **ich** | **breche** | **dich,** |
| boy | spoke | I | pluck | you |

| 'røːs laen | aof | deːʁ | 'hae dən |
|---|---|---|---|
| **Röslein** | **auf** | **der** | **Heiden.** |
| little rose | on | the | heath |

| 'røːs laen | ʃpraːχ | ɪç | 'ʃtɛ çə | dɪç |
|---|---|---|---|---|
| **Röslein** | **sprach:** | **ich** | **steche** | **dich,** |
| little rose | spoke | I | prick | you |

| das | duː | 'eː vɪç | dɛŋkst | an | mɪç |
|---|---|---|---|---|---|
| **dass** | **du** | **ewig** | **denkst** | **an** | **mich,** |
| so that | you | forever | think | of | me |

| ʊnt | ɪç | vɪls | nɪçt | 'lae dən |
|---|---|---|---|---|
| **und** | **ich** | **will's** | **nicht** | **leiden.** |
| and | I | will it | not | suffer |

| 'røːs laen | 'røːs laen | 'røːs laen | roːt |
|---|---|---|---|
| **Röslein,** | **Röslein,** | **Röslein** | **rot,** |
| little rose | little rose | little rose | red |

| 'røːs laen | aof | deːʁ | 'hae dən |
|---|---|---|---|
| **Röslein** | **auf** | **der** | **Heiden.** |
| little rose | on | the | heath |

| ʊnt | deːʁ | 'vɪl də | 'knaː bə | braːχ |
|---|---|---|---|---|
| **Und** | **der** | **wilde** | **Knabe** | **brach** |
| and | the | wild | boy | picked |

| s | 'røːs laen | aof | deːʁ | 'hae dən |
|---|---|---|---|---|
| **'s** | **Röslein** | **auf** | **der** | **Heiden;** |
| the | little rose | from | the | heath |

| 'røːs laen | 'veːr tə | zɪç | ʊnt | ʃtaːχ |
|---|---|---|---|---|
| **Röslein** | **wehrte** | **sich** | **und** | **stach,** |
| little rose | defended | itself | and | pricked |

| half | iːm | dɔχ | kaen | ve: | ʊnt | aχ |
|---|---|---|---|---|---|---|
| **half** | **ihm** | **doch** | **kein** | **Weh** | **und** | **Ach,** |
| helped | it | though | no | woe | and | pain |

| mʊst | ɛs | 'eː bən | 'lae dən |
|---|---|---|---|
| **musst'** | **es** | **eben** | **leiden.** |
| had to | it | just | to suffer |

| 'røːs laen | 'røːs laen | 'røːs laen | roːt |
|---|---|---|---|
| **Röslein,** | **Röslein,** | **Röslein** | **rot,** |
| little rose | little rose | little rose | red |

| 'røːs laen | aof | deːʁ | 'hae dən |
|---|---|---|---|
| **Röslein** | **auf** | **der** | **Heiden.** |
| little rose | on | the | heath |

# Im Frühling

ɪm ˈfryː lɪŋ
**Im Frühling**
in the Spring

ʃtɪl zɪts ɪç an des ˈhyː ɡəls haŋ
**Still sitz ich an des Hügels Hang,**
quiet sit I on the of the hill slope

deːʁ ˈhɪ məl ɪst zoː klar
**der Himmel ist so klar,**
the sky is so clear

das ˈlʏf tçən ʃpiːlt ɪm ˈɡryː nən taːl
**das Lüftchen spielt im grünen Tal,**
the little breeze plays in the green valley

voː ɪç baͤm ˈeːr stən ˈfryː lɪŋs ʃtraːl
**wo ich, beim ersten Frühlingsstrahl,**
where I at the first ray of springtime

aͤnst aχ zoː ˈɡlʏk lɪç vaːʁ
**einst, ach, so glücklich war;**
once ah so happy was

voː ɪç an ˈiː rəʁ ˈzaͤ tə ɡɪŋ
**wo ich an ihrer Seite ging**
where I at her side went

zoː ˈtraͤo lɪç ʊnt zoː naː
**so traulich und so nah,**
so intimately and so near

ʊnt tiːf ɪm ˈdʊn kəln ˈfɛl zən ˌkvɛl
**und tief im dunkeln Felsenquell**
and deep in the dark rock spring

deːn ˈʃøː nən ˈhɪ məl blaͤo ʊnt hɛl
**den schönen Himmel blau und hell**
the beautiful sky blue and bright

ʊnt ziː ɪm ˈhɪ məl zaː
**und sie im Himmel sah.**
and her in the sky saw

ziː viː deːʁ ˈbʊn tə ˈfryː lɪŋ ʃoːn
**Sieh, wie der bunte Frühling schon**
see how the many-colored springtime already

aͤos knɔsp ʊnt ˈblyː tə blɪkt
**aus Knosp' und Blüte blickt,**
from bud and blossom looks

nɪçt ˈa lə ˈblyː tən zɪnt miːʁ ɡlaͤeç
**nicht alle Blüten sind mir gleich,**
not all blossoms are to me alike

am ˈliːp stən pflʏkt ɪç fɔn deːm tsvaͤek
**am liebsten pflückt' ich von dem Zweig,**
at the most liked would pluck I from the branch

fɔn ˈvɛl çəm ziː ɡə ˈpflʏkt
**von welchem sie gepflückt.**
from which she plucked

dɛn ˈa ləs ɪst viː ˈdaː maːls nɔχ
**Denn alles ist wie damals noch,**
for all is as then still

diː ˈbluː mən das ɡə ˈfilt
**die Blumen, das Gefild;**
the flowers the fields

diː ˈzɔ nə ʃaͤent nɪçt ˈmɪn dəʁ hɛl
**die Sonne scheint nicht minder hell,**
the sun shines not less bright

nɪçt ˈmɪn dəʁ frɔͤønt lɪç ʃvɪmt ɪm kvɛl
**nicht minder freundlich schwimmt im Quell**
not less cheerful swims in the spring [water]

das ˈblaͤo ə ˈhɪ məls ˌbɪlt
**das blaue Himmelsbild.**
the blue sky image

ɛs ˈvan dəln nuːʁ zɪç vɪl ʊnt vaːn
**Es wandeln nur sich Will' und Wahn,**
there changes only itself will and illusion

ɛs ˈvɛk səln lʊst ʊnt ʃtraͤet
**es wechseln Lust und Streit,**
there alternates pleasure and strife

fo ˈryː bəʁ fliːt deːʁ ˈli bə ɡlʏk
**vorüber flieht der Liebe Glück,**
past flees of the love happiness

ʊnt nuːʁ diː ˈli bə blaͤept tsu ˈrʏk
**und nur die Liebe bleibt zurück,**
and only the love remains behind

diː liːp ʊnt aχ das laͤet
**die Lieb' und ach, das Leid.**
the love and ah the sorrow

o veːr ɪç dɔχ aͤen ˈfø ɡlaͤen nuːʁ
**O wär ich doch ein Vöglein nur**
o were I but a little bird only

dɔrt an deːm ˈviː zən haŋ
**dort an dem Wiesenhang,**
there on the slope of the meadow

dan bliːb ɪç aͤof deːn ˈtsvaͤe ɡən hiːʁ
**dann blieb ich auf den Zweigen hier**
then would stay I on the branches here

ʊnt zɛŋ aͤen ˈzyː səs liːt fɔn iːʁ
**und säng ein süßes Lied von ihr**
and would sing a sweet song about her

deːn ˈɡan tsən ˈzɔ məʁ laŋ
**den ganzen Sommer lang.**
the whole summer long

# Lachen und Weinen

'la χən  ʊnt  v͡ae nən  tsu:  'je:k lɪ çəʁ  'ʃtʊn də
**Lachen**  **und**  **Weinen**  **zu**  **jeglicher**  **Stunde**
laughing  and  crying  at  every  hour

ru:t  b͡ae  de:ʁ  li:p  a͡of  zo:  'man çəʁ ˌl͡ae  'grʊn də
**ruht**  **bei**  **der**  **Lieb**  **auf**  **so**  **mancherlei**  **Grunde.**
rests  in the case  of  love  upon  so  many a various  cause

'mɔr gəns  la͡χt  ɪç  fo:ʁ  lʊst
**Morgens**  **lacht'**  **ich**  **vor**  **Lust;**
in the morning  laughed  I  for  joy

ʊnt  va 'rʊm  ɪç  nu:n  'v͡ae nə
**und**  **warum**  **ich**  **nun**  **weine**
and  why  I  now  weep

b͡ae  dɛs  'ɑ: bən dəs  'ʃ͡ae nə
**bei**  **des**  **Abendes**  **Scheine,**
at  of the  evening  light

ɪst  mi:ʁ  zɛlp  nɪçt  bə 'vʊst
**ist**  **mir**  **selb'**  **nicht**  **bewusst.**
is  to me  myself  not  known

'v͡ae nən  ʊnt  'la χən  tsu:  'je:k lɪ çəʁ  'ʃtʊn də
**Weinen**  **und**  **Lachen**  **zu**  **jeglicher**  **Stunde**
crying  and  laughing  at  every  hour

ru:t  b͡ae  de:ʁ  li:p  a͡of  zo:  'man çəʁ ˌl͡ae  'grʊn də
**ruht**  **bei**  **der**  **Lieb**  **auf**  **so**  **mancherlei**  **Grunde.**
rests  in the case  of  love  upon  so  many a various  cause

'ɑ: bənds  v͡aent  ɪç  fo:ʁ  ʃmɛrts
**Abends**  **weint'**  **ich**  **vor**  **Schmerz;**
in the evening  wept  I  for  pain

ʊnt  va 'rʊm  du:  ɛʁ 'va χən
**und**  **warum**  **du**  **erwachen**
and  why  you  awake

kanst  am  'mɔr gən  mɪt  'la χen
**kannst**  **am**  **Morgen**  **mit**  **Lachen,**
can  in the  morning  with  laughing

mʊs  ɪç  dɪç  'frɑ: gən  o:  hɛrts
**muss**  **ich**  **dich**  **fragen,**  **o**  **Herz.**
must  I  you  ask  o  heart

# Nacht und Träume

| naχt | ʊnt | ˈtrɔ͡ø mə |
|---|---|---|
| **Nacht** | **und** | **Träume** |
| night | and | dreams |

| ˈha͡el gə | naχt | du: | ˈzɪŋ kəst | ˈni: dər |
|---|---|---|---|---|
| **Heil'ge** | **Nacht,** | **du** | **sinkest** | **nieder!** |
| holy | night | you | sink | down |

| ˈni: dəʁ | ˈva lən | a͡oχ | di: | ˈtrɔ͡ø mə |
|---|---|---|---|---|
| **Nieder** | **wallen** | **auch** | **die** | **Träume,** |
| down | float | also | the | dreams |

| vi: | da͡en | ˈmo:nt lɪçt | dʊrç | di: | ˈrɔ͡ø mə |
|---|---|---|---|---|---|
| **wie** | **dein** | **Mondlicht** | **durch** | **die** | **Räume,** |
| like | your | moonlight | through | the | spaces |

| dʊrç | de:ʁ | ˈmɛn ʃən | ˈʃtɪ lə | brʊst |
|---|---|---|---|---|
| **durch** | **der** | **Menschen** | **stille** | **Brust.** |
| through | of the | human beings | quiet | breast |

| di: | bə ˈla͡o ʃən | zi: | mɪt | lʊst |
|---|---|---|---|---|
| **Die** | **belauschen** | **sie** | **mit** | **Lust,** |
| them | listen to | they | with | pleasure |

| ˈru: fən | vɛn | de:ʁ | tɑ:k | ɛʁ ˈvaχt |
|---|---|---|---|---|
| **rufen,** | **wenn** | **der** | **Tag** | **erwacht:** |
| (they) call | when | the | day | awakes |

| ˈke: rə | ˈvi: dəʁ | ˈha͡el gə | naχt |
|---|---|---|---|
| **kehre** | **wieder,** | **heil'ge** | **Nacht,** |
| return | again | holy | night |

| ˈhɔl də | ˈtrɔ͡ø mə | ˈke: rət | ˈvi: dəʁ |
|---|---|---|---|
| **holde** | **Träume,** | **kehret** | **wieder.** |
| lovely | dreams | return | again |

## Rastlose Liebe

'rast lo: zə   'li: bə
**Rastlose**   **Liebe**
restless   love

de:m   ʃne:   de:m   're: gən
**Dem**   **Schnee,**   **dem**   **Regen,**
the   snow   the   rain

de:m   vɪnt   ɛnt 'ge: gən
**dem**   **Wind**   **entgegen,**
the   wind   in face of

ɪm   dampf   de:ʁ   'klʏf tə
**im**   **Dampf**   **der**   **Klüfte,**
in the   mist   of the   ravines

dʊrç   'ne: bəl ˌdʏf tə
**durch**   **Nebeldüfte,**
through   fog scents

'ɪ məʁ   tsu:   'ɪ məʁ   tsu:
**immer**   **zu,**   **immer**   **zu,**
always   toward   always   toward

'o: nə   rast   ʊnt   ru:
**ohne**   **Rast**   **und**   **Ruh!**
without   rest   and   repose

'li: bəʁ   dʊrç   'lae dən
**Lieber**   **durch**   **Leiden**
rather   through   suffering

mœçt   ɪç   mɪç   'ʃla: gən
**möcht'**   **ich**   **mich**   **schlagen,**
would like   I   myself   to fight

als   zo:   fi:l   'frɔø dən
**als**   **so**   **viel**   **Freuden**
than   so   many   joys

dɛs   'le: bəns   ɛʁ 'tra: gən
**des**   **Lebens**   **ertragen!**
of   life   to endure

'a lə   das   'nae gən
**Alle**   **das**   **Neigen**
all   the   inclining

fɔn   'hɛr tsən   tsu:   'hɛr tsən
**von**   **Herzen**   **zu**   **Herzen,**
of   heart   to   heart

aχ   vi:   zo:   'ae gən
**ach,**   **wie**   **so**   **eigen**
ah   how   so   curiously

'ʃa fət   das   'ʃmɛr tsən
**schaffet**   **das**   **Schmerzen!**
creates   that   pains

vi:   zɔl   ɪç   fli:n
**Wie**   **soll**   **ich**   **fliehn?**
how   should   I   flee

'vɛl dəʁ verts   tsi:n
**Wälderwärts**   **ziehn!**
forestward   to go

'a ləs   fɛʁ 'ge: bəns
**Alles**   **vergebens!**
all   in vain

'kro: nə   dɛs   'le: bəns
**Krone**   **des**   **Lebens,**
crown   of   life

glʏk   'o: nə   ru:
**Glück**   **ohne**   **Ruh,**
happiness   without   peace

'li: bə   bɪst   du:
**Liebe,**   **bist**   **du!**
love   are   you

# Seligkeit

'ze: lɪç kaet
**Seligkeit**
Bliss

'frɔø dən  'zɔn dəʁ  tsa:l
**Freuden  sonder  Zahl**
joys  without  number

bly:n  ɪm  'hɪ məls ˌza:l
**blühn  im  Himmelssaal**
bloom  in the  heaven's hall

'ɛ ŋəln  ʊnt  fɛr 'klɛːʁ tən
**Engeln  und  Verklärten,**
angels  and  transfigured ones

vi:  di:  'fɛː təʁ  'leːʁ tən
**wie  die  Väter  lehrten.**
as  the  fathers  taught

o:  da:  mœçt  ɪç  zaen
**O  da  möcht  ich  sein,**
oh  there  would like  I  to be

ʊnt  mɪç  'e: vɪç  frɔøn
**und  mich  ewig  freun!**
and  myself  forever  to be happy

'je: dəm  'lɛ çəlt  traot
**Jedem  lächelt  traut**
to each  smiles  intimately

'ae nə  'hɪ mels ˌbraot
**eine  Himmelsbraut;**
a  heaven's bride

harf  ʊnt  'psal təʁ  'klɪ ŋət
**Harf  und  Psalter  klinget,**
harp  and  psaltery  sounds

ʊnt  man  tantst  ʊnt  'zɪ ŋət
**und  man  tanzt  und  singet.**
and  one  dances  and  sings

o:  da:  mœçt  ɪç  zaen
**O  da  möcht  ich  sein,**
oh  there  would like  I  to be

ʊnt  mɪç  'e: vɪç  frɔøn
**und  mich  ewig  freun!**
and  myself  forever  to be happy

'li: bəʁ  blaeb ɪç  hiːʁ
**Lieber  bleib ich  hier,**
rather  stay I  here

'lɛ çəlt  'lao ra  miːʁ
**lächelt  Laura  mir**
if smiles  Laura  at me

'ae nən  blɪk  deːʁ  'za: gət
**einen  Blick,  der  saget,**
a  glance  which  says

das  ɪç  'aos gə ˌkla: gət
**dass  ich  ausgeklaget.**
that  I  [have] finished with complaining

'ze: lɪç  dan  mɪt  iːʁ
**Selig  dann  mit  ihr,**
blissful  then  with  her

blaeb ɪç  'e: vɪç  hiːʁ
**bleib ich  ewig  hier!**
stay I  forever  here

# Ständchen

'ʃtɛnt çən
**Ständchen**
Serenade

'la͡e zə 'fle: ən 'ma͡e nə 'li: dɐ
**Leise** **flehen** **meine** **Lieder**
softly entreat my songs

dʊrç di: naχt tsu: di:ɐ
**durch** **die** **Nacht** **zu** **dir,**
through the night to you

ɪn den 'ʃtɪ lən ha͡en hɛɐ 'ni: dɐ
**in** **den** **stillen** **Hain** **hernieder,**
into the quiet grove below

'li:p çən kɔm tsu: mi:ɐ
**Liebchen,** **komm** **zu** **mir.**
sweetheart come to me

'flʏ stɐnt 'ʃlaŋ kə 'vɪp fəl 'ra͡o ʃən
**Flüsternd** **schlanke** **Wipfel** **rauschen**
whispering slender treetops rustle

ɪn dɛs 'mo:n dəs lɪçt
**in** **des** **Mondes** **Licht,**
in the of the moon light

dɛs fɛɐ 'rɛ: tɐs 'fa͡ent lɪç 'la͡o ʃən
**des** **Verräters** **feindlich** **Lauschen**
of betrayer hostile eavesdropping

'fʏrç tə 'hɔl də nɪçt
**fürchte,** **Holde,** **nicht.**
fear lovely one not

høːrst di: 'naχ tɪ ˌga lən 'ʃla: gən
**Hörst** **die** **Nachtigallen** **schlagen?**
hear you the nightingales beat

aχ zi: 'fle: ən dɪç
**Ach!** **sie** **flehen** **dich,**
ah they entreat you

mɪt de:ɐ 'tø: nə 'sy: sən 'kla: gən
**mit** **der** **Töne** **süßen** **Klagen**
with of the tones sweet lamenting

'fle: ən zi: fy:ɐ mɪç
**flehen** **sie** **für** **mich.**
entreat they for me

zi: fɛɐ 'ʃte:n dɛs 'bu: zəns 'ze: nən
**Sie** **verstehn** **des** **Busens** **Sehnen,**
they understand of the bosom yearning

'kɛ nən 'li: bəs ˌʃmɛrts
**kennen** **Liebesschmerz,**
(they) know of love pain

'ry: rən mɪt den 'zɪl bɐ ˌtø: nən
**rühren** **mit** **den** **Silbertönen**
(they) touch with the silver tones

'je: dəs 'va͡e çə hɛrts
**jedes** **weiche** **Herz.**
every soft heart

las a͡oχ di:r di: brʊst bə 've: gən
**Lass** **auch** **dir** **die** **Brust** **bewegen,**
let also to you the breast be moved

'li:p çən 'hø: rə mɪç
**Liebchen,** **höre** **mich!**
sweetheart hear me

'be: bənt har ɪç di:r ɛnt 'ge: gən
**Bebend** **harr** **ich** **dir** **entgegen,**
trembling wait I to you toward

kɔm bə 'glʏ kə mɪç
**komm,** **beglücke** **mich.**
come make happy me

# An die Musik

Franz von Schober
(1796–1882)

Franz Schubert
(1797–1828)

D 547. Original key: D major. Schubert and the young law student and poet Schober met in 1815 and collaborated on this song in March, 1817 when both were twenty years old. At the time, Schubert was living in the Schober home; his friend would provide him with lodgings on other occasions as well, in 1822, 1826, and 1827–28. Schober had the opportunity to introduce the composer to the noted baritone Johann Vogl (1768–1840), who became the most significant singer to perform and promote Schubert's songs among the wider public. The original tempo indication on the autograph is *Etwas bewegt* [Somewhat agitated], but for publication Schubert changed it to *Mässig* [Moderate]. The song was published in 1827 as Op. 88, No. 4 by Thaddäus Weigl of Vienna, and for this occasion Schubert also slightly altered the music, adding the grace note in bar 5 and changing the bass line in bars 4 and 13. Schubert set 12 Schober poems. Schober was for a time, well after Schubert's death, secretary to Franz Liszt.

| An die Musik | To Music |
|---|---|
| Du holde Kunst, in wieviel grauen Stunden, | *You lovely art, in how many gloomy hours,* |
| Wo mich des Lebens wilder Kreis umstrickt, | *when life's fierce orbit entangled me,* |
| Hast du mein Herz zu warmer Lieb entzunden, | *have you kindled my heart to warmer love,* |
| Hast mich in eine bessre Welt entrückt. | *have you carried me away to a better world.* |
| | |
| Oft hat ein Seufzer, deiner Harf entflossen, | *Often has a sigh, flown from your harp—* |
| Ein süßer, heiliger Akkord von dir, | *a sweet, holy chord from you—* |
| Den Himmel bessrer Zeiten mir erschlossen, | *unlocked for me the heaven of better times.* |
| Du holde Kunst, ich danke dir dafür, | *You lovely art, I thank you for this.* |
| Du holde Kunst, ich danke dir. | *You lovely art, I thank you.* |

Le - bens wil - der Kreis um - strickt, hast du mein
hei - li - ger Ak - kord_ von_ dir, den Him - mel

Herz__ zu__ war - mer Lieb ent - zun - den, hast mich in ei - ne
bess - rer__ Zei - ten mir er - schlos - sen, du hol - de Kunst, ich__

cresc.

bess - re Welt ent - rückt, in ei - ne bess - re Welt__ ent - rückt.
dan - ke dir da - für, du hol - de Kunst,__ ich dan - ke dir.

[>] p

fp fp

# An die Nachtigall

Matthias Claudius
(1740–1815)

Franz Schubert
(1797–1828)

D 497. Original key: G major. Schubert's song was probably composed in November, 1816. It was not published until 1829. There is a striking similarity between "An die Nachtigall" and "An die Geliebte," composed 13 months earlier and possessing a nearly identical theme. Matthias Claudius was a theology student, later turning to political science and law before becoming a poet (publishing under the pseudonym Asmus) and the editor of the *Wandsbecker Bote* (Wandsbeck Messenger). In later life he returned to religion as his major interest. This poem was written in 1771, with the original title "Nachtigall, Nachtigall, ach!"

| An die Nachtigall | To the Nightingale |
|---|---|
| Er liegt und schläft an meinem Herzen, | *He lies and sleeps upon my heart;* |
| Mein guter Schutzgeist sang ihn ein; | *my good guardian spirit sang him to sleep.* |
| Und ich kann fröhlich sein und scherzen, | *And I can be joyful and can have fun—* |
| Kann jeder Blum und jedes Blatts mich freun. | *can delight in every flower and every leaf.* |
| Nachtigall, ach! Nachtigall, ach! | *Nightingale, ah! Nightingale, ah!* |
| Sing mir den Amor nicht wach! | *Do not sing my love awake!* |

# Auf dem Wasser zu singen

Friedrich Leopold Graf zu Stolberg
(1750–1819)

Franz Schubert
(1797–1828)

D 774. Original key: A-flat major. This song first appeared as a supplement to the *Wiener Zeitschrift für Kunst, Literatur, Theater und Mode* in 1823 in the key of A-flat major, based on a copy now in the Witteczek-Spaun collection. Schubert's autograph copy is lost. The poem by Stolberg was written in honor of the poet's widely admired first wife and titled "Lied auf dem Wasser zu singen. Für meine Agnes." [Song to be sung upon the water. For my Agnes.] This is one of nine Stolberg poems set by Schubert. The supple, shimmering figuration in the piano right hand is paralleled in the vocal line, underpinning the theme of radiance that permeates the verse.

| Auf dem Wasser zu singen | *To Be Sung on the Water* |
|---|---|
| Mitten im Schimmer der spiegelnden Wellen<br>Gleitet, wie Schwäne, der wankende Kahn.<br>Ach, auf der Freude sanft schimmernden Wellen<br>Gleitet die Seele dahin wie der Kahn. | *Midst the shimmer of mirroring waves*<br>*glides, like swans, the rocking boat.*<br>*Ah, on joy's softly shimmering waves*<br>*glides the soul along, like the boat.* |
| Denn von dem Himmel herab auf die Wellen<br>Tanzet das Abendrot rund um den Kahn.<br>Über den Wipfeln des westlichen Haines<br>Winket uns freundlich der rötliche Schein.<br>Unter den Zweigen des östlichen Haines<br>Säuselt der Kalmus im rötlichen Schein. | *For from the heaven above, upon the waves*<br>*dances the sunset round about the boat.*<br>*Above the treetops of the western grove*<br>*beckons to us kindly the rosy glow.*<br>*Beneath the branches of the eastern grove*<br>*rustles the iris in the rosy glow.* |
| Freude des Himmels und Ruhe des Haines<br>Atmet die Seel im errötenden Schein.<br>Ach, es entschwindet mit tauigem Flügel<br>Mir auf den wiegenden Wellen die Zeit.<br>Morgen entschwindet mit schimmerndem Flügel<br>Wieder wie gestern und heute die Zeit,<br>Bis ich auf höherem strahlenden Flügel<br>Selber entschwinde der wechselnden Zeit. | *Joy of heaven, and peace of the grove*<br>*breathes the soul in the reddening glow.*<br>*Alas, time vanishes on dewy wing*<br>*for me upon the lulling waves.*<br>*Tomorrow time will vanish with shimmering wing*<br>*again, as yesterday and today,*<br>*until I upon loftier, more radiant wings*<br>*myself vanish in the flux of time.* |

Mit - ten im Schim - mer der spie - geln - den Wel - len glei - tet, wie Schwä - ne, der
Ü - ber den Wip - feln des west - li - chen Hai - nes win - ket uns freund - lich der
Ach, es ent - schwin - det mit tau - i - gem Flü - gel mir auf den wie - gen - den

wan - ken - de Kahn.
röt - li - che Schein.
Wel - len die Zeit.

Ach, auf der Freu - de sanft schim - mern - den Wel - len
Un - ter den Zwei - gen des öst - li - chen Hai - nes
Mor - gen ent - schwin - det mit schim - mern - dem Flü - gel

15

[cresc.]  [p]

glei - tet die See - le da - hin wie der Kahn, ach, auf der Freu - de sanft
säu - selt der Kal - mus im röt - li - chen Schein, un - ter den Zwei - gen des
wie - der wie ges - tern und heu - te die Zeit, mor - gen ent - schwin - det mit

cresc.

p

18

[cresc.]

schim - mern - den Wel - len glei - tet die See - le da - hin wie der Kahn.
öst - li - chen Hai - nes säu - selt der Kal - mus im röt - li - chen Schein.
schim - mern - dem Flü - gel wie - der wie ges - tern und heu - te die Zeit,

cresc.

21

[p]

Denn von dem Him - mel her - ab auf die Wel - len
Freu - de des Him - mels und Ru - he des Hai - nes
bis ich auf hö - he - rem strah - len - den Flü - gel

p

tan - zet das A - bend-rot rund um den Kahn, tan -
at - met die Seel im er - rö - ten-den Schein, at -
sel - ber ent-schwin - de der wech - seln-den Zeit, sel -

[*f*]

- zet das A - bend-rot rund um den Kahn.
- met die Seel im er - rö - ten-den Schein.
- ber ent - schwin - de der wech - seln-den Zeit.

*f*

[ ] *p* [ ]

*fp*

[ ]

1., 2.

3.

*decresc.*

# Die Forelle

Christian Friedrich Daniel Schubart
(1739–1791)

Franz Schubert
(1797–1828)

D 550. Original key: D-flat major. Between 1817 and 1821, Schubert made no fewer than five versions of the song "Die Forelle" (The Trout). Only the last version of 1821 includes the piano introduction that so vividly exposes the pictorial idea of the lapping water and darting trout. An earlier version inspired an amateur cellist to commission the "Trout" piano quintet (1819) from Schubert, wherein the song theme is used as the basis for an Andantino set of decorative variations in the fourth movement. The poet and musician Schubart is remembered principally as founder of the Augsberg journal *Die deutsche Chronik* and for his poetry's connection to Schubert's music. The poet was politically outspoken and served ten years in prison for his ideas which had culminated in a satirical attack on the duke of Württemberg and his mistress.

Die Forelle

In einem Bächlein helle,
Da schoss in froher Eil
Die launische Forelle
Vorüber wie ein Pfeil.
Ich stand an dem Gestade
Und sah in süßer Ruh
Des muntern Fischleins Bade
Im klaren Bächlein zu.

Ein Fischer mit der Rute
Wohl an dem Ufer stand
Und sah's mit kaltem Blute,
Wie sich das Fischlein wand.
So lang dem Wasser Helle,
So dacht ich, nicht gebricht,
So fängt er die Forelle
Mit seiner Angel nicht.

Doch endlich ward dem Diebe
Die Zeit zu lang. Er macht
Das Bächlein tückisch trübe,
Und eh ich es gedacht,
So zuckte seine Rute,
Das Fischlein zappelt dran,
Und ich mit regem Blute
Sah die Betrogne an.

*The Trout*

*In a clear brook*
*there darted in joyful haste*
*the capricious trout*
*passed, like an arrow.*
*I stood on the bank*
*and watched, in sweet peace,*
*the merry little fish's bath*
*in the clear brook.*

*A fisherman with his rod*
*stood right at the edge*
*and observed, heartlessly,*
*how the little fish wriggled around.*
*As long as the clearness of the water—*
*so thought I—is not lacking,*
*then he won't catch the trout*
*with his hook.*

*But finally became, for the thief,*
*the waiting time too long. He made*
*the little brook, maliciously, muddy;*
*and before I realized it,*
*he jerked his rod.*
*The little fish struggled on it;*
*and I, with quick pulse,*
*regarded the betrayed one.*

22

muntern Fisch-leins Ba - de im kla - ren Bäch-lein zu.
fängt er die_ Fo-rel - le mit sei - ner An-gel nicht.

26

1.

Ein

30

2.

Doch end-lich ward dem Die - be die Zeit zu

cresc.

34

lang. Er macht das Bäch-lein tü-ckisch

p

cresc.

trü - be, und eh_____ ich es ge - dacht, so zuck - te sei - ne

Ru - te, das Fisch - lein, das Fisch - lein zap - pelt dran, und

ich mit re - gem Blu - te sah die Be - trog - ne an, und

ich__ mit re - gem__ Blu - te sah die Be - trog - ne an.

# Du bist die Ruh

Friedrich Rückert
(1788–1866)

Franz Schubert
(1797–1828)

D 776. Original key: E-flat major. Rückert, the poet for six of Schubert's songs, was influenced by the Persian poet Hafis (1325–1389) and was a scholar of eastern languages. He taught in both Erlangen and Berlin. When authoring his 1821 collection of poetry titled *Östlichen Rosen* [Eastern Roses] he left the verses untitled, and Schubert therefore gave the name "Du bist die Ruh" to this song. Rückert later gave the poem a title drawn from the third stanza, "Kehr' ein bei mir" [Commune with me]. This song and two others on Rückert texts (see "Lachen und Weinen") were published as Op. 59 in September of 1826 by Sauer and Leidesdorf. This text allowed Schubert to group stanzas into a three-part modified strophic form, and the reverent transcendence of the verse finds perfect poise in the music's balance of quietude and intensity.

| Du bist die Ruh | You Are Rest |
|---|---|
| Du bist die Ruh, | You are rest, |
| Der Friede mild, | gentle peace; |
| Die Sehnsucht du, | the longing, you, |
| Und was sie stillt. | and that which satisfies it. |
| | |
| Ich weihe dir | I consecrate to you, |
| Voll Lust und Schmerz | full of joy and sorrow, |
| Zur Wohnung hier | as a dwelling place here, |
| Mein Aug und Herz. | my eyes and heart. |
| | |
| Kehr ein bei mir, | Come commune with me, |
| Und schließe du | and close |
| Still hinter dir | quietly behind you |
| Die Pforten zu. | the gates. |
| | |
| Treib andern Schmerz | Drive other pain |
| Aus dieser Brust. | from this breast. |
| Voll sei dies Herz | Full may this heart be |
| Von deiner Lust. | of your joy. |
| | |
| Dies Augenzelt, | The temple of these eyes |
| Von deinem Glanz | from your radiance |
| Allein erhellt, | alone brightens; |
| O füll es ganz. | oh, fill it completely. |

was sie stillt. Ich wei - he dir___ voll_ Lust und_ Schmerz

zur Woh - nung hier___ mein Aug_ und_ Herz,___ mein Aug und_ Herz.___

pp

Kehr ein bei mir, und schlie - ße du still hin - ter dir die

(legato)

Pfor - ten zu. Treib an - dern Schmerz___ aus_ die - ser___ Brust.

Voll sei dies Herz___ von dei - ner___ Lust,___ von dei - ner___ Lust.___

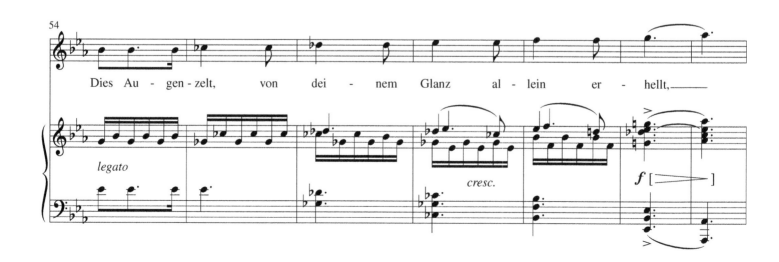

Dies Au - gen - zelt, von dei - nem Glanz al - lein er - hellt,___

# Ganymed

Johann Wolfgang von Goethe
(1749–1832)

Franz Schubert
(1797–1828)

D 544. Original key: A-flat major. In the mythological story, Ganymede was carried to heaven by an eagle, as commanded by Zeus. The beautiful youth was to be a cup bearer for the gods. Goethe's poem was written in 1774. "Ganymed" was composed in March, 1817, and published in 1825 by Diabelli, as Opus 19, No. 3. The original tempo marking, *Etwas geschwind* [Somewhat fast], was changed to *Etwas langsam* [Somewhat slow]. While this change was probably Schubert's, the published dedication to Goethe was made without Schubert's permission. It is believed that this song firmed the friendship between Schubert and the talented baritone, Johann Michael Vogl. Vogl (1768–1840) was a popular singer in Vienna and the most important Schubertian singer of his time. Schubert first heard his talents in a performance as Orestes in *Iphigénie en Tauride* in 1813. At their first meeting, in 1817, Schubert showed the baritone three songs, and from that time considered him the ideal interpreter of his work. Schubert once wrote to his brother, Ferdinand, "The way and manner in which Vogl sings and I accompany, so that we seem in such a moment to be one, is something quite new and unheard of to these people." Vogl premiered "Erlkönig" before its 1821 publication, and shortly before his death performed *Winterreise* in its entirety. He died on the twelfth anniversary of Schubert's death.

| Ganymed | Ganymede |
|---|---|
| Wie im Morgenglanze | *How, in the morning's splendor,* |
| Du rings mich anglühst, | *you glow all around me,* |
| Frühling, Geliebter! | *spring, beloved!* |
| Mit tausendfacher Liebeswonne | *With love's thousandfold rapture* |
| Sich an mein Herze drängt | *presses upon my heart* |
| Deiner ewigen Wärme | *your eternal warmth's* |
| Heilig Gefühl, | *divine feeling,* |
| Unendliche Schöne! | *endless beauty!* |
| Dass ich dich fassen möcht | *Would that I could hold you* |
| In diesen Arm! | *in these arms!* |
| | |
| Ach, an deinem Busen | *Ah, at your breast* |
| Lieg ich, und schmachte, | *I lie and languish;* |
| Und deine Blumen, dein Gras | *and your flowers, your grass* |
| Drängen sich an mein Herz. | *press against my heart.* |
| Du kühlst den brennenden | *You cool the burning* |
| Durst meines Busens, | *thirst of my bosom,* |
| Lieblicher Morgenwind! | *lovely morning breeze!* |
| Ruft drein die Nachtigall | *Therein calls the nightingale* |
| Liebend nach mir aus dem Nebeltal. | *lovingly to me from the misty valley.* |
| Ich komm! ich komme! | *I come, I come!* |
| Ach! wohin? wohin? | *Ah, whither? Whither?* |
| | |
| Hinauf strebt's, hinauf! | *Upward I soar, upward!* |
| Es schweben die Wolken | *The clouds float* |
| Abwärts, die Wolken | *downward; the clouds* |
| Neigen sich der sehnenden Liebe. | *bow down to yearning love—* |
| Mir! Mir! | *to me! To me!* |
| In eurem Schoße | *Into your lap,* |
| Aufwärts! | *upwards!* |
| Umfangend umfangen! | *Embracing, embraced!* |
| Aufwärts an deinen Busen, | *Upwards to your bosom,* |
| Allliebender Vater! | *all-loving Father!* |

25
Wär - me hei - lig Ge - fühl, un - end -

29
- li - che Schö - ne! Dass ich dich fas - sen möcht

34
in die - sen Arm! Ach, an dei - nem Bu - sen lieg ich, und

39
schmach - te, und dei - ne Blu - men, dein Gras drän -

gen sich an— mein Herz.

Du kühlst den bren - nen-den Durst mei - nes Bu - sens,

lieb - li - cher Mor - gen - wind!

Ruft drein die

# Der Musensohn

Johann Wolfgang von Goethe
(1749–1832)

Franz Schubert
(1797–1828)

D 764. Original keys: A-flat major and G major. This is one among the seventy-four settings the composer made of the texts of this great German poet and author. (See "Gretchen am Spinnrade" and "Rastlose Liebe.") Schubert composed this song in A-flat major in 1822 along with three other Goethe settings (D 764–767), all dedicated to Josef von Franck. Changes, probably made by the publisher M. J. Leidesdorf when releasing the set in 1828, include altering the key to G major and numbering the collection as Op. 92, rather than the earlier mistaken designation of Op. 87. The accompaniment has the perpetual motion quality often favored by Schubert, here enlivened through the use of syncopation.

Der Musensohn

Durch Feld und Wald zu schweifen,
Mein Liedchen wegzupfeifen,
So geht's von Ort zu Ort.
Und nach dem Takte reget
Und nach dem Maß beweget
Sich alles an mir fort.

Ich kann sie kaum erwarten,
Die erste Blum im Garten,
Die erste Blüt am Baum.
Sie grüßen meine Lieder,
Und kommt der Winter wieder,
Sing ich noch jenen Traum.

Ich sing ihn in der Weite,
Auf Eises Läng' und Breite,
Da blüht der Winter schön.
Auch diese Blüte schwindet,
Und neue Freude findet
Sich auf bebauten Höhn.

Denn wie ich bei der Linde
Das junge Völkchen finde,
Sogleich erreg ich sie.
Der stumpfe Bursche bläht sich,
Das steife Mädchen dreht sich
Nach meiner Melodie.

Ihr gebt den Sohlen Flügel
Und treibt durch Tal und Hügel
Den Liebling weit von Haus.
Ihr lieben, holden Musen,
Wann ruh ich ihr am Busen
Auch endlich wieder aus?

*The Muses' Son*

*Through field and wood roaming,*
*whistling my little song,*
*so I go from place to place.*
*And in time to my beat*
*and in measure moves*
*everything past me.*

*I can hardly wait for them:*
*the first flower in the garden,*
*the first blossom on the tree.*
*They greet my songs;*
*and when winter comes again,*
*I still sing my former dream.*

*I sing it far and wide,*
*upon the length and breadth of the ice,*
*there blossoms winter beautifully!*
*This blossom also vanishes,*
*and new joy is found*
*on the tilled highlands.*

*Then as I, by the linden*
*find the young folk,*
*at once I inspire them.*
*The dull fellow puffs himself up,*
*the awkward girl whirls*
*to my tune.*

*You give my feet wings*
*and propel over valley and hill*
*your favorite one far from home.*
*You dear, gracious muses,*
*when shall I repose upon her breast*
*finally, again?*

**Ziemlich lebhaft**

*p* — *fp* [>]

Durch Feld und Wald zu schwei - fen, mein Lied - chen weg - zu -

pfei - fen, so geht's von Ort zu Ort, so geht's von Ort— zu Ort. Und

nach dem Tak - te re - get und nach dem Maß be - we - get sich al - les an— mir

fort,_____ und nach dem Maß be - we - get sich al - les an mir fort.

Ich

kann sie kaum er - war - ten, die ers - te Blum im Gar - ten, die ers - te

Blüt am____ Baum. Sie grü - ßen mei - ne Lie - der, und

40

kommt der Win - ter wie - der, sing ich noch je - nen___ Traum, sing

45

ich___ noch je - nen,___ je - nen Traum. Ich

[cresc.]

50

sing ihn in der Wei - te, auf Ei - ses Läng' und Brei - te, da

*mf*

54

blüht der Win - ter schön, da blüht der Win - ter schön. Auch die - se Blü - te

schwin - det, und neu - e Freu - de fin - det sich auf be - bau - ten

Höhn,____ und neu - e Freu - de fin - det sich auf be - bau - ten Höhn.

Denn

wie ich bei der Lin - de das jun - ge Völk - chen fin - de, so - gleich er -

Lieb - ling weit von Haus, den Lieb - ling weit von Haus. Ihr lie - ben, hol - den

Mu - sen, wann ruh ich ihr am Bu - sen auch end - lich wie - der aus, _____ wann

ruh ich ihr am Bu - sen auch end - lich wie - der aus?

# Heidenröslein

Johann Wolfgang von Goethe
(1749–1832)

Franz Schubert
(1797–1828)

D 257. Original key: D major. One of five Goethe songs written on August 19, 1815, this was published by Cappi and Diabelli as Opus 3, No. 3 in May, 1821. Three other Goethe settings ("Schäfers Klagelied," "Meeres Stille," and "Jägers Abendlied II") complete Opus 3, all dedicated "with great respect" to Ignaz von Mosel, assistant director of the court theaters in Vienna. Goethe is generally considered to be the greatest of German poets. His vast output (133 volumes) encompasses poems, novels, plays, scientific studies, a famous correspondence with Schiller, and the 12,000 line *Faust*, written over a period of 60 years. Though he never received acknowledgement or approval from Goethe, Schubert set 74 of his poems to music.

Heidenröslein

Sah ein Knab ein Röslein stehn,
Röslein auf der Heiden,
War so jung und morgenschön,
Lief er schnell, es nah zu sehn,
Sah's mit vielen Freuden.
Röslein, Röslein, Röslein rot,
Röslein auf der Heiden.

Knabe sprach: ich breche dich,
Röslein auf der Heiden.
Röslein sprach: ich steche dich,
Dass du ewig denkst an mich,
Und ich will's nicht leiden.
Röslein, Röslein, Röslein rot,
Röslein auf der Heiden.

Und der wilde Knabe brach
's Röslein auf der Heiden;
Röslein wehrte sich und stach,
Half ihm doch kein Weh und Ach,
Musst' es eben leiden.
Röslein, Röslein, Röslein rot,
Röslein auf der Heiden.

*Little Heath Rose*

*A lad saw a wild rose,*
*wild rose on the heath.*
*It was so young, and lovely as morning.*
*He ran quickly to look at it closely;*
*he looked at it with much joy.*
*Wild rose, wild rose, wild rose red,*
*wild rose on the heath.*

*The lad said, "I will pick you,*
*wild rose on the heath!"*
*The wild rose said, "I will prick you,*
*so that you will always remember me;*
*and I will not suffer from it."*
*Wild rose, wild rose, wild rose red,*
*wild rose on the heath.*

*And the impetuous lad picked*
*the wild rose on the heath.*
*The wild rose defended itself and pricked,*
*but grief and pain was of no avail;*
*it had to suffer after all.*
*Wild rose, wild rose, wild rose red,*
*wild rose on the heath.*

Hei - den, war so jung und mor - gen - schön,
Hei - den. Rös - lein sprach: ich ste - che dich,
Hei - den; Rös - lein wehr - te sich und stach,

lief er schnell, es nah zu sehn, sah's mit vie - len
dass du e - wig denkst an mich, und ich will's nicht
half ihm doch kein Weh und Ach, musst' es e - ben

*nachgebend*

Freu - den. Rös - lein, Rös - lein, Rös - lein rot,
lei - den. Rös - lein, Rös - lein, Rös - lein rot,
lei - den. Rös - lein, Rös - lein, Rös - lein rot,

*pp*

*wie oben*

Rös - lein auf der Hei - den.
Rös - lein auf der Hei - den.
Rös - lein auf der Hei - den.

*cresc.*

# Im Frühling

Ernst Konrad Friedrich Schulze
(1789–1817)

Franz Schubert
(1797–1828)

D 882. Original key: G major. The poem comes from Schulze's *Poetisches Tagebuch* [Verse Journal], and was retitled by Schubert. The first version was written in March, 1826, with *Langsam* [Slow] as the tempo marking. It was first published in the Weiner *Zeitschrift für Kunst, Literatur, Theater und Mode* in September of 1828. Later that year it appeared as the first of the four songs in Opus 101. Schulze's fiancé died before their marriage; his poetry reflects this youthful tragedy. Schulze died young of tuberculosis.

Im Frühling

Still sitz ich an des Hügels Hang,
Der Himmel ist so klar,
Das Lüftchen spielt im grünen Tal,
Wo ich, beim ersten Frühlingsstrahl,
Einst, ach, so glücklich war;

Wo ich an ihrer Seite ging
So traulich und so nah,
Und tief im dunkeln Felsenquell
Den schönen Himmel blau und hell
Und sie im Himmel sah.

Sieh, wie der bunte Frühling schon
Aus Knosp' und Blüte blickt,
Nicht alle Blüten sind mir gleich,
Am liebsten pflückt' ich von dem Zweig,
Von welchem sie gepflückt.

Denn alles ist wie damals noch,
Die Blumen, das Gefild;
Die Sonne scheint nicht minder hell,
Nicht minder freundlich schwimmt im Quell
Das blaue Himmelsbild.

Es wandeln nur sich Will' und Wahn,
Es wechseln Lust und Streit,
Vorüber flieht der Liebe Glück,
Und nur die Liebe bleibt zurück,
Die Lieb' und ach, das Leid.

O wär ich doch ein Vöglein nur
Dort an dem Wiesenhang,
Dann blieb ich auf den Zweigen hier
Und säng ein süßes Lied von ihr
Den ganzen Sommer lang.

*In the Springtime*

*Quietly I sit on the hillside.*
*The sky is so clear.*
*The zephyr plays in the green valley*
*where I, in the first rays of springtime*
*once, alas, was so happy,*

*where I at her side walked*
*so intimately and so close,*
*and deep in the dark rock's spring*
*saw the beautiful heavens, blue and bright,*
*and saw her in the heavens.*

*See how the colorful springtime already*
*appears from bud and blossom!*
*Not all blossoms are the same to me;*
*I like best to pick from the branch*
*from which she picked.*

*For all is still as it was in those days:*
*the flowers, the fields;*
*the sun shines no less brightly,*
*no less cheerfully floats in the spring*
*the blue heavens' image.*

*Only will and illusion change;*
*pleasure alternates with strife.*
*Away flies love's happiness,*
*and only the love remains behind—*
*the love and, alas, the sorrow.*

*Oh, were I but only a little bird*
*there on the meadow's slope;*
*then I would stay in the branches here*
*and sing a sweet song about her*
*all summer long.*

Still sitz ich an des Hü - gels Hang, der Him - mel ist_ so_ klar, das

Lüft-chen spielt im_ grü - nen Tal, wo ich, beim ers-ten Früh-lings-strahl, einst, ach, so_ glück-lich war, so_glück-lich

war; wo ich an ih - rer Sei - te_ ging so trau-lich und so nah, und

tief im dun-keln Fel - sen-quell den schö - nen Him-mel blau und hell und sie im Him-mel sah, und_

sie im Him-mel sah.

*pp*

Sieh, wie der bun - te Früh - ling schon aus

Knosp' und Blü - te blickt, Nicht al - le Blü - ten sind mir gleich, am

liebs - ten pflückt' ich von dem Zweig, von wel - chem sie ge-pflückt, von wel-chem sie ge-

*ppp*

35 wan - deln nur sich Will' und Wahn, es wech - seln Lust und Streit, vor -

37 ü - ber flieht der Lie - be Glück, und nur die Lie - be bleibt zu-rück, die

39 Lieb' und ach, das Leid, und ach, das Leid.

41 O wär ich doch ein Vög - lein nur dort

# Lachen und Weinen

Friedrich Rückert
(1788–1866)

Franz Schubert
(1797–1828)

D 777. Original key: A-flat major. Schubert titled this song "Lachen und Weinen" [Laughter and Weeping] as Rückert had left the poem untitled when it appeared in his 1821 collection *Östlichen Rosen* [Eastern Roses]. Schubert composed the song almost certainly during the summer of 1822, although it was not published until Sauer and Leidesdorf released it alongside two other Rückert settings in September of 1826. (See "Du bist die Ruh.") When authoring this collection of poetry, Rückert was strongly influenced by and even consciously imitating the works of the Persian poet Hafis (1325–1389). Goethe experienced a similar attraction to the works of Hafis at about the same time. One hallmark of Schubert's expressivity is very evident in this setting: the use of major and minor tonal fluctuations, sometimes within just one or two measures, to reflect the way the composer felt the slightest changes of mood or meaning within the poem.

| Lachen und Weinen | Laughter and Weeping |
|---|---|
| Lachen und Weinen zu jeglicher Stunde | Laughter and weeping, at whatever hour, |
| Ruht bei der Lieb auf so mancherlei Grunde. | are based, in the case of love, on so many different reasons. |
| Morgens lacht' ich vor Lust; | Every morning I laughed for joy; |
| Und warum ich nun weine | and why I now weep |
| Bei des Abendes Scheine, | in the evening's glow |
| Ist mir selb' nicht bewusst. | is even to myself unknown. |
| | |
| Weinen und Lachen zu jeglicher Stunde | Weeping and laughter, at whatever hour, |
| Ruht bei der Lieb auf so mancherlei Grunde. | are based, in the case of love, on so many different reasons. |
| Abends weint' ich vor Schmerz; | Evenings I have wept for sorrow; |
| Und warum du erwachen | and how can you wake up |
| Kannst am Morgen mit Lachen, | in the morning with laughter, |
| Muss ich dich fragen, o Herz. | must I ask you, oh heart. |

Stun - de ruht bei der Lieb auf so man - cher - lei Grun - de.

Mor - gens lacht' ich vor Lust; und wa -

rum ich nun wei - ne bei des A - ben - des

Schei - ne, ist mir selb' nicht be - wusst, ist mir selb' nicht be -

35

wusst.

41

47

Wei - nen und La - chen zu jeg - li - cher Stun - de ruht__ bei der

53

Lieb__ auf so man - cher - lei Grun - de. A - bends weint' ich vor

Schmerz;_____ und wa - rum du er - wa - chen kannst am Mor - gen mit

*cresc.*

La - chen, muss ich dich fra - gen, o Herz, muss ich dich fra - gen, o

Herz.

*pp*

# Nacht und Träume

Matthäus von Collin
(1779–1824)

Franz Schubert
(1797–1828)

D 827. Original key: B major. Schubert set five poems by Collin in 1822–23. Collin was a professor of philosophy in Cracow and Vienna, tutor to Napoleon's son, and a cousin of Josef von Spaun (1788–1865). Spaun was Schubert's schoolmate at Vienna's *Stadtkonvict* and ultimately the first person of wide influence to recognize Schubert's genius and promote publication of the songs. Through Spaun the composer became acquainted with Mayrhofer, Wogl, Schober and Witteczek, all of whom were important in Schubert's artistic growth. Spaun's *Memoirs* offers us important insights into Schubert's life. It was Spaun's idea to have Schubert's songs published in a series of volumes arranged by poet. Collin's poem was not published until 1827, so Schubert had access to a manuscript copy. The first publication of the song in 1825 as Op. 43, No. 2 erroneously named Schiller as the poet. In the Spaun family collection there is a slightly different version marked not *Sehr langsam* [Very slow] but rather *Langsam, Sempre legato* [Slow, Always legato].

Nacht und Träume

Heil'ge Nacht, du sinkest nieder!
Nieder wallen auch die Träume,
Wie dein Mondlicht durch die Räume,
Durch der Menschen stille Brust.
Die belauschen sie mit Lust,
Rufen, wenn der Tag erwacht:
Kehre wieder, heil'ge Nacht,
Holde Träume, kehret wieder.

*Night and Dreams*

*Hallowed night, you sink down!*
*Downward float also the dreams,*
*like your moonlight, through space,*
*through the silent bosom of people.*
*They listen to you with pleasure—*
*cry out, when the day breaks:*
*Come back, hallowed night;*
*lovely dreams, come back.*

durch der_ Men - schen stil - le, stil - le Brust. Die be-

lau - schen sie_ mit_ Lust, die be - lau - schen sie_ mit_ Lust,

ru - fen, wenn der Tag er-wacht: Keh - re wie-der, heil'-ge Nacht, hol - de Träu-me, keh-ret

wie - der, hol - de_ Träu - me, keh - ret wie - der.

# Rastlose Liebe

Johann Wolfgang von Goethe
(1749–1832)

Franz Schubert
(1797–1828)

D 138. Original keys: E major and D major from two autograph sources. Schubert's seventy-four settings of texts by Goethe reveal a great variety of musical approaches and remarkable sensitivity to poetic nuance. Schubert composed this song on May 19, 1815, dedicated to his teacher Anton Salieri. It was published by Cappi and Diabelli in July of 1821 as Op. 5, No. 1. The song was received enthusiastically in a performance by the composer at the home of Count Erdody on July 13, 1816. Schubert recorded this event in his diary and continued, "one cannot deny that Goethe's musical and poetic genius was largely responsible for the applause." Goethe wrote this poem in May of 1771 while staying in the Thuringian Forest in the wake of a snowstorm. Schubert's agitated sixteenth-note accompanimental figure drives the music forward, as in "Gretchen am Spinnrade," but here the pain and restlessness of love is paradoxical, an element of the mood of extreme joy which bursts forth in the several repetitions of the final phrases.

| Rastlose Liebe | Restless Love |
|---|---|
| Dem Schnee, dem Regen, | Against the snow, the rain, |
| Den Wind entgegen, | the wind, |
| Im Dampf der Klüfte, | in the mist of the ravines, |
| Durch Nebeldüfte, | through foggy vapors, |
| Immer zu, immer zu, | ever onward, ever onward, |
| Ohne Rast und Ruh! | without repose or rest! |
| | |
| Lieber durch Leiden | Rather through suffering |
| Möcht' ich mich schlagen, | would I fight my way, |
| Als so viel Freuden | than to bear |
| Des Lebens ertragen! | so much of life's joy! |
| Alle das Neigen | All the inclining |
| Von Herzen zu Herzen, | of heart to heart— |
| Ach, wie so eigen | ah, how it in its own way |
| Schaffet das Schmerzen! | creates pain! |
| | |
| Wie soll ich fliehn? | How shall I flee? |
| Wälderwärts ziehn! | Go toward the forest? |
| Alles vergebens! | All in vain! |
| Krone des Lebens, | Crown of life, |
| Glück ohne Ruh, | happiness without rest, |
| Liebe, bist du! | love, are you! |

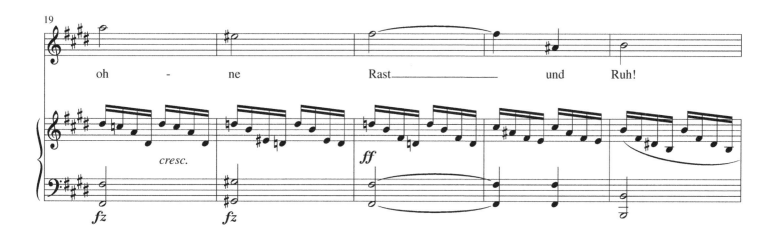

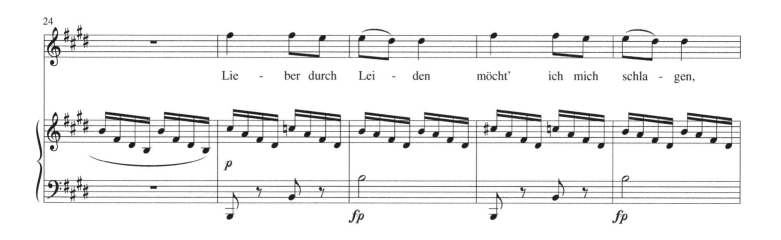

als so_____ viel\_\_ Freu - den des Le - bens er -

tra - gen! Al - le das Nei - gen von Her - zen zu

Her - zen, ach, wie so ei - gen schaf - fet das

Schmer - zen! Wie soll ich fliehn? Wäl - der - wärts

72

# Gretchen am Spinnrade

Johann Wolfgang von Goethe
(1749–1832)

Franz Schubert
(1797–1828)

D 118. Original key: D minor. Goethe is widely recognized as the greatest figure in German poetry and one of history's towering intellects. His 12,000-line verse drama *Faust*, in which this poem appears as the scene "Gretchens Stube" (Gretchen's Room), was written over a period of some 60 years. Schubert set this text on October 19, 1814, and even as a teenager conjured one of the great miniature masterpieces in all of song literature. This was the first Goethe poem that Schubert set, and was eventually published by Cappi and Diabelli in April of 1821 as Opus 2. In this scene, Gretchen is abandoned by her lover Faust, who has made a pact with the devil, Mephistopheles. The driving, spinning wheel motif in the piano and strong harmonic motion contribute to the song's dramatic intensity. Schubert altered the first line of the last verse of the poem on its repeat to "O könnt' ich ihn küssen" (Oh, if I could kiss him). Though Schubert never received the slightest approval or even acknowledgement from Goethe when published songs were sent to him, the composer set 74 of his poems to music.

Gretchen am Spinnrade

*Gretchen at the Spinning Wheel*

Meine Ruh ist hin,
Mein Herz ist schwer,
Ich finde sie nimmer
Und nimmermehr.

*My peace is gone,
my heart is heavy;
I will find it never
and nevermore.*

Wo ich ihn nicht hab,
Ist mir das Grab,
Die ganze Welt
Ist mir vergällt.

*Wherever I do not have him
is for me the grave;
the whole world
is to me loathsome.*

Mein armer Kopf
Ist mir verrückt,
Mein armer Sinn
Ist mir zerstückt.

*My poor head
is deranged;
my poor mind
is shattered.*

Nach ihm nur schau ich
Zum Fenster hinaus,
Nach ihm nur geh ich
Aus dem Haus.

*For him only do I gaze
out from the window;
For him only do I go
out of the house.*

Sein hoher Gang,
Sein' edle Gestalt,
Seines Mundes Lächeln,
Seiner Augen Gewalt,

*His fine gait,
his noble stature,
his mouth's smile,
his eyes' power,*

Und seiner Rede
Zauberfluss,
Sein Händedruck,
Und ach, sein Kuss!

*and, of his speech,
magic flow—
his handclasp,
and, ah, his kiss!*

Mein Busen drängt
Sich nach ihm hin,
Ach dürft' ich fassen
Und halten ihn,

*My bosom yearns
for him;
ah, could I embrace him
and hold him,*

Und küssen ihn,
So wie ich wollt',
An seinen Küssen
Vergehen sollt'.

*and kiss him
as much as I wish,
in his kisses
I should perish.*

geh ich aus_____ dem Haus. Sein ho - her

Gang,_____ sein' ed - le Ge - stalt, sei - nes Mun - des

Lä - cheln, sei - ner Au - gen Ge - walt, und sei - ner

Re - de Zau - ber - fluss, sein

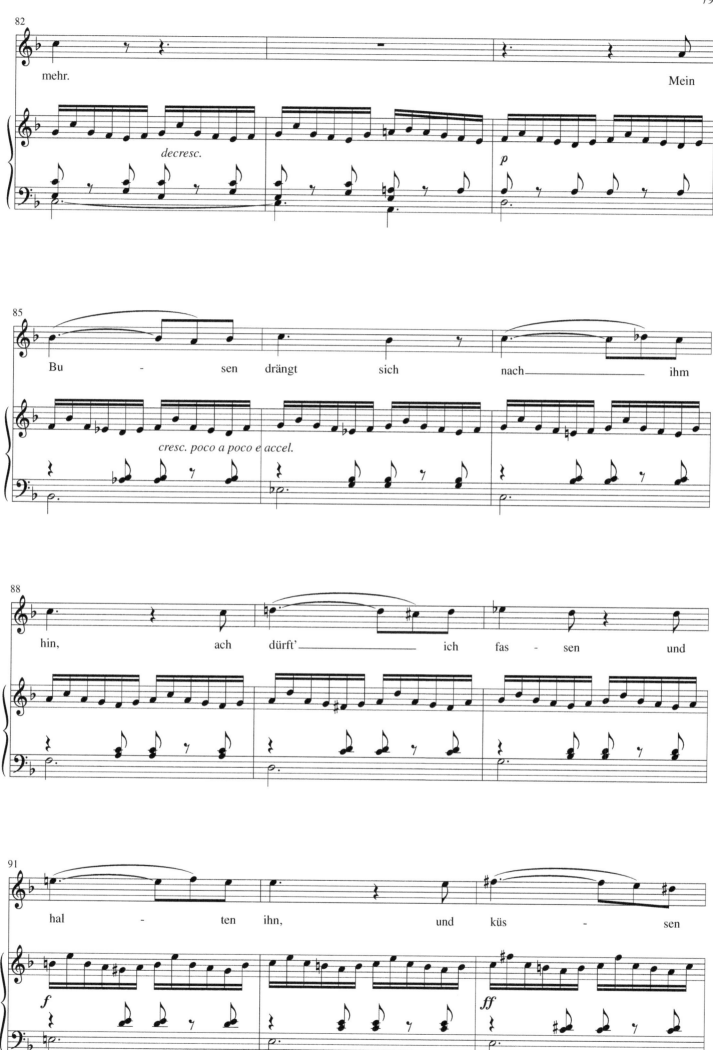

# Seligkeit

Ludwig Christoph Heinrich Hölty
(1748–1776)

Franz Schubert
(1797–1828)

D 433. Original key: E major. The poem dates from 1773. The song was composed in May of 1816 but remained unpublished until 1895. It is a traditional lieder encore. Schubert set 23 Hölty poems, all but one from 1815–1816. Hölty, along with others, founded the Gottinger Dichterbund, a society of young poets. Though educated in theology, Hölty never entered the clergy. He died of consumption in Hanover, the city of his birth.

Seligkeit

Freuden sonder Zahl
Blühn im Himmelssaal
Engeln und Verklärten,
Wie die Väter lehrten.
O da möcht ich sein,
Und mich ewig freun!

Jedem lächelt traut
Eine Himmelsbraut;
Harf und Psalter klinget,
Und man tanzt und singet.
O da möcht ich sein,
Und mich ewig freun!

Lieber bleib ich hier,
Lächelt Laura mir
Einen Blick, der saget,
Dass ich ausgeklaget.
Selig dann mit ihr,
Bleib ich ewig hier!

*Bliss*

*Joys without number*
*bloom in heaven's hall*
*for angels and transfigured ones,*
*as our fathers taught.*
*Oh, there should I like to be,*
*and forever rejoice!*

*Upon everyone smiles intimately*
*a heavenly bride;*
*harp and psalter sound,*
*and one dances and sings.*
*Oh, there should I like to be,*
*and forever rejoice!*

*Rather will I stay here,*
*if Laura smiles upon me*
*a glance which says*
*that I've been freed from complaining.*
*Blissful then with her*
*will I remain forever here!*

# Ständchen

Ludwig Rellstab
(1799–1860)

Franz Schubert
(1797–1828)

D 957, No. 4. Original key: D minor. Schubert completed seven songs on poems by Rellstab in August of 1828, three months before his death. This is the fourth of that set. He hoped to see the songs published, an event that occurred only posthumously after his brother Ferdinand sold the songs along with six settings of Heine's poetry to the publisher Tobias Haslinger. Haslinger recognized these, along with one late setting of Seidl, as significant in Schubert's song output, calling them, "the last blossoming of his noble art" and released all fourteen works under the title *Schwanengesang* [Swan Song] in May 1829. This is the second song of Schubert's to have the popular German Romantic title "Ständchen" [Serenade]; the earlier, also known as "Horch, horch, die Lerch" [D 889] was written in 1826. The staccato eighth notes in the piano introduction and similar figurations throughout mimic the plucking of the serenader's guitar, an instrument for which Schubert had great affinity. Poet Rellstab was a trained pianist who was in his twenties when both Beethoven and Schubert grew enthusiastic about his poetry.

| Ständchen | Serenade |
|---|---|
| Leise flehen meine Lieder | *Gently plead my songs* |
| Durch die Nacht zu dir, | *through the night to you;* |
| In den stillen Hain hernieder, | *into the quiet grove below,* |
| Liebchen, komm zu mir. | *sweetheart, come to me.* |
| | |
| Flüsternd schlanke Wipfel rauschen | *Whispering, slender treetops rustle* |
| In des Mondes Licht, | *in the moon's light;* |
| Des Verräters feindlich Lauschen | *of a betrayer's unfriendly eavesdropping* |
| Fürchte, Holde, nicht. | *be not afraid, lovely one.* |
| | |
| Hörst die Nachtigallen schlagen? | *Do you hear the nightingales' call?* |
| Ach! sie flehen dich, | *Ah, they implore you;* |
| Mit der Töne süßen Klagen | *with the sound of sweet laments* |
| Flehen sie für mich. | *they plead to you for me.* |
| | |
| Sie verstehn des Busens Sehnen, | *They understand the heart's longing;* |
| Kennen Liebesschmerz, | *they know love's pain.* |
| Rühren mit den Silbertönen | *They stir, with silvery tones,* |
| Jedes weiche Herz. | *every tender heart.* |
| | |
| Lass auch dir die Brust bewegen, | *Let your heart also be moved;* |
| Liebchen, höre mich! | *sweetheart, hear me!* |
| Bebend harr ich dir entgegen, | *Trembling, I await you;* |
| Komm, beglücke mich. | *come, make me happy.* |

**Mäßig**

Lei - se fle - hen mei - ne Lie - der durch die Nacht zu dir,
Hörst die Nach - ti - gal - len schla - gen? Ach! sie fle - hen dich,

*stacc.*

in— den stil - len Hain her-nie - der,
mit— der Tö - ne sü - ßen Kla - gen

Lieb - chen, komm zu mir.
fle - hen sie— für mich.

Flüs - ternd schlan - ke Wip - fel rau - schen in— des Mon - des Licht,
Sie ver - stehn des Bu - sens Seh - nen, ken - nen Lie - bes - schmerz,

*pp*

mich! Be - bend harr ich dir ent-ge - gen,

komm, be-glü - cke mich, komm, be-glü - cke

mich, be - glü - cke mich.